DARBON, LESLIE
TIME TO KILL. A PLAY. [BY]
LESLIE DARBON.
822.914   23-329530

TIME TO KILL

A play

LESLIE DARBON

SAMUEL FRENCH

LONDON
NEW YORK   TORONTO   SYDNEY   HOLLYWOOD

© 1979 by Leslie Darbon

This play is fully protected under the Copyright Laws of the British Commonwealth of Nations, the United States of America and all countries of the Berne and Universal Copyright Conventions.

All rights, including Stage, Motion Picture, Radio, Television, Public Reading, and Translation into Foreign Languages, are strictly reserved.

No part of this publication may lawfully be transmitted, stored in a retrieval system, or reproduced in any form or by any means, electronic, mechanical, photocopying, manuscript, typescript, recording, or otherwise, without the prior permission of the copyright owners.

Rights of Performance by Amateurs are controlled by SAMUEL FRENCH LTD, 26 SOUTHAMPTON STREET, LONDON WC2E 7JE, and they, or their authorized agents, issue licences to amateurs on payment of a fee. **It is an infringement of the Copyright to give any performance or public reading of the play before the fee has been paid and the licence issued.**

Licences are issued subject to the understanding that it shall be made clear in all advertising matter that the audience will witness an amateur performance; that the names of the authors of the plays shall be included on all announcements and on all programmes; and that the integrity of the author's work will be preserved.

The Royalty Fee indicated below is subject to contract and subject to variation at the sole discretion of Samuel French Ltd.

> Basic fee for each and every
> performance by amateurs   Code L
> in the British Isles

In Theatres or Halls seating Six Hundred or more the fee will be subject to negotiation.

In Territories Overseas the fee quoted above may not apply. A fee will be quoted on application to our local authorized agent, or if there is no such agent, on application to Samuel French Ltd, London.

The Professional Rights in this play are controlled by HARVEY UNNA & STEPHEN DURBRIDGE LTD, 14 Beaumont Mews, Marylebone High Street, London W1.

The publication of this play does not imply that it is necessarily available for performance by amateurs or professionals, either in the British Isles or Overseas. Amateurs and professionals considering a production are strongly advised in their own interests to apply to the appropriate agents for consent before starting rehearsals or booking a theatre or hall.

ISBN 0 573 11445 5

CHARACTERS

Don Parkes
Maggie Parkes
Helen Francis
Alan Sexton
Jane Abbott
Liz Thomas

The action takes place in the house of Don and Maggie Parkes on the Riverside Park Estate, near Maidenhead

ACT I
    Scene 1   Morning
    Scene 2   Fifteen minutes later

ACT II   Fifteen minutes later

Time—the present

ACT I

Scene 1

An elegant modern house on the Riverside Park Estate, bordering the River Thames, near Maidenhead. Morning

Built about seven years ago their original cost was between twenty and twenty-five thousand pounds. They are almost double that price now. They are the homes of business executives, directors, the successful self-employed—people in the higher income bracket. This house belongs to Don and Maggie Parkes. Like the others it is designed as an open-plan unit to give a feeling of space and light. The living-room area and the dining-room area are, in fact, all in one. But, it is very well thought out so that although the two areas are integral, they appear to be separate from each other. After the first scene the set is dressed—very simply and with the aid of only a minimum of props—to represent a court room. Consequently, the layout of this set needs to take this into consideration to help achieve this aim with as little fuss as possible. To one side is the main front door and entrance to the house. Either side of the door is a window which looks out on to the drive and the front lawn. Sweeping down to the front door is a staircase. Only the lower part of it is seen, but it forms an important part of the set since when it reaches the front door it follows the line of a landing and curls out into the living-room area. Set in this small landing area is a heavy wrought-iron chair, which is clearly garden furniture and looks conspicuously out of place. At the extreme end of this landing two steps lead down into the living-room itself. The living-room area is furnished with taste and elegance. The odd button-backed chair in different and varied shapes is dotted around. There is a small and attractive Chesterfield. The feeling is one of comfortable elegance. The general furniture and furnishings are period and, consequently, the opposite to what might be expected. There is, for instance, the clean cut Swedish look which the house would seem to dictate. So, the contrast of period furniture in such a modern setting is immediately noticeable and striking. There is a bookcase that is also a cunningly concealed drinks bar. In fact, the bar is a Victorian bow-fronted chest in rich, dark mahogany with its back removed so that drinks and glasses can be stored there whilst being readily accessible. This bow-front chest stands away from the bookcase so that it is possible to move behind it and serve drinks. The only concession this bar makes to the modern era is two high-backed bar stools. On either side of the bookcase are windows to allow for maximum light. On the other side is the dining area. From it a door leads into the kitchen. Beside this door there is a long hatch which also serves as a breakfast counter. This is filled with a laminated shutter which when pulled down forms an attractive mosaic very similar to the old Victorian mosaic brooches. When down it becomes an attractive mural. It is gravity weighted so that it is very easy to pull up and down. Indeed, it can have quite a dramatic effect if given a quick shove, for it will shoot up "like a rocket". Under the stairs there is a cupboard and this is used mainly for outdoor clothing. Maggie also keeps her laundry basket here—clothes that have already been washed and are waiting to be ironed

As the CURTAIN rises, Don Parkes comes down the stairs to the main living-room. He is dressed in his trousers, but is shirtless; he appears irritated. Don Parkes is in his late thirties; a deep person, known on the estate and in business as a quiet man. Because of this people tend to underestimate him, believing him to be a weak person. He is anything but. He is a man of some strength and determination. He can be trusted with any secret, any confidence; he plays things very close to his chest. He is a man to be reckoned with, not to be underestimated. He can be dangerous and vindictive if the mood takes him. He is a very successful man, and this in itself should be a clue to his character and his strength—and a warning as to his resourcefulness. However, he has a way of hiding all this—of deceiving others. Apart from being successful in business he is also successful with women; but he keeps a very low profile where this side of his nature is concerned. He is a director of an international electronics company. He is a Cambridge law graduate but could see no quick way to the top of his field so, like many of his contemporaries, he opted for a business and commercial career

At the bottom of the stairs he stops and has a look out of the window by the door

Don Where the hell are you, Maggie? (*As he turns, he notices the wrought-iron chair and frowns at it—no more, just to register it. He turns away from the window and rubs his bare chest before moving down into the living-room. He goes to the cupboard under the stairs and opens the door. A pile of laundry that must be all of six feet high falls down around his feet. He looks at it, appalled*) Shit! (*He drops to his knees and starts to pick it up and hurl it back into the cupboard: but he comes across a shirt he clearly has not seen in years*) Christ! (*He hurls it back into the cupboard and finishes the job quickly before closing the door and leaning against it in relief and partly because he is afraid the whole lot is going to fall out again. He tentatively moves away from the door and it remains closed. He looks around the room and spots his suitcase open on the bow-front chest/bar. He goes to it and at first takes out a large manilla folder. For a moment he is side-tracked by this. He does not open it. But he stands there smiling at it. Clearly it is something special. He gives it "a quick kiss for luck" then replaces it before taking out several other items—probably underwear—but is unable to find a shirt. He then moves behind the chest and opens a drawer in the lower part of the bookcase and takes out a camera. He is about to put this into the suitcase when he notices that some of the books are out of place. Clearly, he is irritated by this and he almost casually drops the camera into the suitcase before turning back to the bookcase to give his full attention to straightening up the books. He takes* *them all out and rearranges them in the order they should be in and to his own satisfaction. Having done this, he moves from behind the bow-front chest/bar and crosses to the dining-table on which we see a tray containing various items such as a glass, a milk jug, a packet of unprocessed bran, a jar of honey and some teaspoons)*

The front door opens and Maggie Parkes enters. Maggie, like Don, is an honours graduate but has used her degree and her intellect very little lately for reasons that will become apparent. She has chosen to be just a housewife at the moment. So—she is bored. But, she has in no way become boring. She is extremely well-read and keeps abreast of current affairs. Her interests include the theatre, fine arts and antiquities. Apart from charm and taste and her clear and obvious academic talents she also has one really great asset. She is a born leader. She has little trouble getting others to follow her lead. Her background is upper middle class. She was born deep in the heart of Tory-held Surrey, of well-off parents and is a very right-wing thinker. She believes in an almost fascist form of meritocracy. You get from life only that which you are prepared to put into it. A dustman is a dustman because he wants to be a dustman. If he wanted to be something else he'd get out and try to improve himself. Self-improvement is high on her list of virtues. On a personal level she is a woman with a great deal of love in her—perhaps too much since she is inclined to be very possessive. She demands a lot from those she loves. Outwardly, Maggie gives the appearance of being a reasonably happy and contented person, but there's a whole saucepan of problems underneath waiting to boil over. Don senses this—and to avoid triggering off an eruption he keeps the conversation light and breezy. Nevertheless, the tension comes across

Don *Ah.* There you are.
Maggie (*crossing*) You're not wearing a shirt.
Don (*looking at himself*) You noticed.

She smiles and slips her arms around him

Maggie If this is a ploy to get me back into bed so that you can have your evil way with me—forget it. I've got the ironing to do.
Don (*breaking from her*) What is it about ironing. I get the impression you're not very fond of doing it.
Maggie I *adore* doing it. The reason I don't do it very often is to deprive myself of the pleasure. Deprivation builds character. You can have too much of a good thing, you know.
Don Well—give yourself a treat, eh? Run a hot iron over a shirt for me, please.
Maggie Have you looked in the kitchen.

He taps his head with the flat of his hand as a gesture of disgust with himself

I thought you hadn't. There are four in there. Crisp. Clean. Beautifully ironed. And waiting for someone to take occupation.
Don Sorry, love. I'll get them.
Maggie No, don't worry. I'll do it. I want to pack three of them anyway.

She goes to the kitchen. A moment. Then the hatch slides up and she tosses him a shirt

Maggie It's a bit damp. Hopefully you'll only get a mild case of pneumonia.
Don Oh, ta.

He puts the shirt on and buttons it up as Maggie returns from the kitchen and goes to the suitcase on the bar/bow-front chest. She places the shirts carefully into the case

Where have you been?
Maggie It's Thursday.
Don Good.
Maggie My turn to take the kids to school.
Don Maggie—we haven't got any kids.
Maggie True. (*She looks down at herself and pats her tummy*) We haven't even got one cooking.

He moves to her and holds her close

Don Remember those wonderful weekends in Brighton before we were married?
Maggie The ones my mother believed we were spending at the Youth Fellowship Hostel?
Don Mmmm.
Maggie I remember.
Don Those nights of endless passion . . .
Maggie When I discovered you snored . . .
Don And we agreed that we didn't want children. They would limit us.
Maggie You believed me, did you?
Don (*he holds her out at arms length*) You weren't lying to me, were you?
Maggie Sort of . . .
Don Well, I wasn't lying to you.
Maggie I know. (*She pulls away from him*) I'd better make sure you've got everything. (*She looks into his case and holds up a camera*) Some business trip.
Don Well—it's the first time I've been to Cologne.
Maggie Oh. By the way—you'll need some new sheets for your album soon.
Don Could you get me some while I'm away, please?

She nods agreement

Maggie (*after a moment*) Would you consider doing something for me?
Don (*suspiciously*) Anything.
Maggie Move?
Don Move?
Maggie Us. From here.
Don But you love it here.
Maggie I'd like to go somewhere where nobody knows us.

Act I, Scene 1

Don You'd be lonely. We're like one big happy family on this estate.
Maggie We—all know each other too well.
Don We're friends. We'd miss the social life. There's the Golf Club. The Drama Society. Bridge. They're our kind of people. If we move away well, there's no telling who we might land up with as neighbours.
Maggie A change might be good for us . . .
Don You don't like change . . .

For a brief moment, a slight edge creeps in

Maggie You don't!

He moves close to her again

Don (*sympathetically*) What is it? What's gone wrong? Did something happen while you were out?
Maggie (*after a moment*) As I came past Rosemary's house just now the postman was coming away. Someone is still sending her letters. They don't know.
Don Oh, you poor darling.

He draws her close to him

Things like this are always going to happen. I know she was a good friend. But, she wouldn't want you to get uptight like this. You've got to put it behind you.
Maggie It's not easy . . .
Don (*after a moment*) Perhaps you need help . . .
Maggie How could anyone leave her . . . to die.
Don Now, you don't know that, Maggie. It's pure fantasy—and it's got to stop.
Maggie I *saw* her.
Don (*sighing*) Well, even supposing you're right, there isn't anything you can do about it.
Maggie Isn't there?
Don What exactly do you mean by that?
Maggie Oh, nothing . . .
Don Well, there isn't! So don't lose any more sleep over it.

In an effort to change the subject Don closes his suitcase and moves with it to the front door where he leaves it ready for when he goes

Maggie You're off now, are you?
Don As soon as my taxi arrives.
Maggie Oh.
Don My plane doesn't leave till eleven thirty.
Maggie You won't be here when the girls arrive for coffee, will you?
Don No way! (*A pause*) I wondered why you were trying to get rid of me.
Maggie (*quickly*) I wasn't.

He goes back to her

Don It sounded as if you were.

There is a slight pause

Maggie I love you . . .
Don If you are trying to get rid of me, you're not actually going the right way about it.

She gives a little laugh

Don That's better.

Suddenly he remembers something. His reaction startles her

Don I've got a bone to pick with you.
Maggie Oh?

He goes to the bookcase

Don Who's been mucking about with my text books?
Maggie Which books?
Don The ones the company gave me. I can't see what anyone else could possibly find of interest in them.
Maggie Oh, it was young Gary. Liz's boy. Something to do with school. You don't mind, do you?
Don I'd be obliged if he put them back in the right order. And I sincerely hope his interest in electricity is purely academic. Because if a young kid like that starts mucking about with it he could electrocute himself.
Maggie I don't think he'd do anything silly.
Don (*rather harshly*) Make sure!
Maggie (*snapping*) I'm not mad. I know you think I am. But, I'm not. I don't need to see a psychiatrist.
Don No, of course you don't.
Maggie That's what you were hinting at a minute or so ago.
Don No, I wasn't, sweetheart . . . you misunderstood me . . .
Maggie How do you think it would affect you? If you'd walked into her house and found her lying there—murdered.

There is a slight pause

Don Murdered?
Maggie *Someone* left her there to die. *Someone* who could have saved her.
Don Even if that is true—it still doesn't make it murder. You know very well that didn't come into the police investigations.
Maggie My father would have known what to do . . .

She trails off knowing what kind of reaction this will have on Don

Don Oh, he would. Captain Bligh would know exactly what to do.

A pause

Maggie is considering whether to continue or not. She decides to go on.

Maggie When he took command of his first ship—there was a spate of stealing on board. Eventually they found who was doing it and the

Act I, Scene 1

ratings set up a court. Put the thief on trial. Found him guilty. And tossed him overboard.
Don So he got a soaking.
Maggie It was winter. The middle of the Atlantic. He could only have lasted a minute or two.
Don (*sceptically*) Are you serious?
Maggie Never more . . .
Don And that's what your father would do, is it? If he caught this imaginary person—the one you think left Rosemary to die.
Maggie I told you about it to illustrate a point.
Don Which is?
Maggie That sometimes it's necessary to take drastic action for the good of the majority. After that little incident . . .
Don *Little incident?*
Maggie . . . anyone could leave anything lying around on that ship. And no one would touch it. You see, everyone realized they had to respect each other's person—and property . . . there were no more fights . . . no one interfered with anyone else's life . . . and the ship ran smoothly from that moment on.
Don Oh, come off it, Maggie love. I don't believe a word of this story. It's another one of your father's stirring sea sagas that won't stand up to close scrutiny. And, anyway, you would have told me about it years ago if it had really happened.
Maggie He swore me to secrecy.
Don But, if what you're saying is true—it was *murder*.
Maggie Oh, yes. Cry murder now—when it suits you. But, the fact is, it worked. It may be rough—but, I call it justice.

A pause

Are you suitably shocked?
Don I was just thinking. How much harder women are than men. Only when a man talks about justice—he means fair play. But, when a woman talks about justice—she means retribution.
Maggie I agree. We're much more ruthless than men. You've got a soft streak in you. It's sentimentality, I suppose. We're not like that at all.

A pause

Don't go, darling . . .

But Don is still deep in his thoughts

Don Eh?
Maggie Please don't go. To Cologne.
Don Maggie, I've got to. It's the biggest deal I've ever handled. If I can get them to sign that contract . . . I must be next in line for the Managing Director's job.
Maggie Oh, goody, goody. That'll put me on equal terms with Liz.
Don Huh! We all know how she managed to catch Bill, don't we? (*He slips an arm around her*) It'll be all right.

Maggie (*nodding*) I suppose so.
Don Where's that bloody taxi?

He goes to the front door, opens it and looks out. Because of its position he is forced to register the wrought-iron chair

Don (*indicating the chair*) What's this doing here?
Maggie Nothing.
Don I can see that. But, what's it doing here?
Maggie Well, it's been languishing around here ever since you and your mates got sloshed and nicked it from the Golf Club.
Don I did explain why. It's a trophy.
Maggie And have I not begged, pleaded and occasionally asked you to return it?
Don There have been several discussions on those lines, yes.
Maggie Well, I can't wait any longer. I'm throwing it out.
Don What?

He makes a dash to "defend" his trophy and is about to pick it up when she stops him

Maggie It's a joke. (*Laughing*) I was pulling your leg.

He reluctantly moves away from it and we see the relief on her face

Don You're in a funny mood today. Woe betide anyone who crosses you.

The front door bell rings

Maggie (*with obvious relief*) That'll be your taxi.

Don opens the door

    Helen Francis is standing outside. She is an attractive lady in her midthirties. She is a very highly strung person; of nervous disposition; tentative in action as well as speech. She is the sort of person that is usually dominated by others. On the other hand, she is also one of those persons who if pushed to the edge of the precipice, can be very dangerous indeed. She is married to Joe Francis who is a chemist and has a very successful business in Maidenhead. She is very much under his influence mainly because she came from a "lower strata" of society and it shows at the edges

Don (*surprised*) Oh Helen . . .
Helen Hello, Don. Oh. I, er—thought you'd be gone . . .
Don No. We thought you were my taxi.

Maggie moves to them

Maggie Come in, Helen. Don's ready to leave. You're not interrupting anything.

Helen enters and Don closes the door behind her. As she moves down into the living-room, he takes his jacket off the bentwood hat- and coat-stand by the landing and puts it on ready to leave. It can be seen that there is also a raincoat there. Don follows Helen into the living-room area

Helen I—I've only popped in for a moment. You see—I've got an appointment at the doctor's this morning . . .
Don Oh.
Helen I keep getting these terrible headaches . . .
Maggie Couldn't Joe give you something for it?
Helen He did. He even went back to the shop at midnight. But, nothing seems to work. I didn't sleep a wink and Joe's fed up with me waking him up so he thinks it best if I go to the doctor.
Maggie What time's your appointment?
Helen The thing is—that's why I called in. You see—I may not be able to get away in time . . .
Maggie You can't let us down now. Everything's arranged.
Don (*very friendlily*) We know your coffee's fabulous, darling—but, if Helen's at the doctor's she can hardly be here as well . . .
Maggie But if you don't turn up it'll spoil everything. Come on, Helen. You can't let us down now. Everything's arranged.

There is a slight edge in Maggie's voice which Helen notices

Don So re-arrange it for next week. Do the *ironing* today.
Maggie Ho-ho! He can't understand why women hate ironing, Helen. I'm relying on you to turn up and get me out of it.
Helen Well . . .
Maggie Come on—make up the four. We can't play bridge with only three of us. It'll do your headache good.
Don Perhaps you ought to, Helen. Otherwise they might decide to play some other sort of game.
Maggie Now there's a veiled comment if ever I've heard one.
Don Oh, come on, Maggie. Everybody around here knows what's been going on at these coffee mornings.
Maggie I've no idea what you're on about. Have you, Helen?

Clearly, Helen feels very awkward

Helen Well . . .
Don All right, Maggie. I'll just have to refresh your memory. Let's take last week for instance. You and your friends got together and decided—wouldn't it be jolly to go along to the Littlewick Council Estate. Pose as Jehovah's Witnesses—and wheedle your way into their homes . . .
Maggie Really. Where did you hear such a ridiculous story?
Don Helen knows.
Helen Me . . .
Don Your husband told me all about it on Sunday morning—down at *The Duke*. He was very upset. (*To Maggie*) I'm not too delighted myself. But, you've had such a lot to contend with recently—I decided to let it pass . . .
Maggie But, you haven't . . .

Don No. (*Pause*) And just in case you're thinking of blaming Helen for Joe finding out, one of the women you harangued with your pseudo-religious fervour was so upset she had to see her doctor. Joe made up her prescription and she told him all about it. She recognized poor Helen . . .

A taxi approaches and the horn sounds loudly several times. This breaks up any further argument on the subject

Maggie There's your taxi, darling. (*She smiles at him, knowing that he has lost his opportunity*)

Don How very convenient. (*He picks up his suitcase and then moves back to Maggie. He kisses her gently and quickly*) I'll be back by Saturday lunchtime. Be a good girl. (*He goes up on the landing*)

Maggie I always am.

Don takes the light raincoat off the bentwood hat- and coat-stand. Just before making his exit he turns to her and smiles

Don Do me a favour.
Maggie Anything . . .
Don Stick to bridge. It's safer. That's right, isn't it, Helen?

Helen has not been expecting this to be tossed at her. She gives a nervous little laugh in reply

Maggie Safe home.
Don Thanks. (*He is about to exit, but pauses*) Tell me one thing. Was it you who nailed the pig's head to the wall of the Men Only bar at the Golf Club?
Maggie (*brightly*) Perish the thought.
Don 'Bye. (*A pause*) Love you.
Maggie Love you, too. 'Bye.

Don exits

Was it Joe who told Don about the pig's head?
Helen No, I'm sure it wasn't. Joe was suspicious but he didn't dare ask me about that. Don was guessing, I'm sure.
Maggie You sound very certain.
Helen Joe is the Golf Club captain.
Maggie Yes. He wouldn't like anyone to find out, would he.
Helen I've got to go, Maggie.
Maggie I'll see you later.
Helen Joe'll kill me if he ever finds out.

Maggie takes her by the shoulders

Maggie He mustn't find out, must he? We've got to keep it to ourselves this time.
Helen I don't know I'm sure.
Maggie Tell you what. We'll make this the very last time.
Helen Well—if it really is the last.

Act I, Scene 1

Maggie Promise. (*A slight pause*) You wouldn't want to miss it, anyway.
Helen I'll see . . .

Helen moves away and goes to the door with Maggie close behind her

Maggie (*casually*) Oh, by the way. You did get the spirits of salt for me, didn't you?

Helen stops—a look of fear on her face

Helen Joe wasn't very happy about it. He was going to ask Don why you needed it . . .
Maggie What?
Helen But, I lied and told him Don had already gone to Cologne.
Maggie (*again trying to be casual*) Well, it wouldn't have mattered anyway. I only want it to clean some badly corroded brass.
Helen Well he doesn't normally sell it over the counter. They won't sell it to you at Boots.
Maggie Which is why I asked you to get it for me.
Helen It's highly dangerous—you could burn yourself badly.
Maggie I'll be extra careful. (*Ushering her through the front door*) Bring it with you when you come back.

Helen nods meekly, and exits

'Bye.
Helen (*off*) 'Bye.

Maggie closes the door behind her, pauses briefly as if in thought, then crosses quickly to the telephone and dials

Maggie (*into the receiver*) Jane. . . . Maggie. Look, love, Helen's got a touch of the fearfuls. I think Joe's had a go at her. The thing is—she's likely to chicken out. Perhaps we should forget it. What do you think? . . . She's at the doctor's. . . . Well, if you're convinced it's the only way. I'll leave it to you. . . . I'm sorry if I don't sound so enthusiastic, but I suppose I'm not looking forward to—well, you know—what I've got to do. . . . There's no need to worry—I won't let you down. Look—I must go. 'Bye. (*She replaces the receiver and checks her watch, then crosses to the wrought-iron chair on the landing. She bends down and from under the carpet she pulls out the end of a length of cable. The positive and negative wires have already been prepared so that they can be wired to either arm of the chair. She does this, feeding them along the arms and down the legs—taping them so that they are difficult to see if looked at casually. Then she tucks the "spare" cable back under the carpet. She goes to the door which leads into the kitchen. She stops, bends down, lifts the carpet and takes out the other end of the cable which has a small connecting socket on it*)

She exits into the kitchen for a moment and returns with another length of wire which she connects up to the socket, before placing it carefully back under the carpet

The front doorbell rings. She looks across at the front door—slightly irritated—brushes her hair with her hands, smoothes her skirt, then goes and opens the door

>*Alan Sexton stands outside. He is thirty-five plus: a handsome man who is a little over-weight, but you would not notice unless you were up close. He is the sort of person about whom it is said: "In a few years' time he'll be really fat if he doesn't watch it." However, he knows he's a "good-looking feller". And he goes out of his way to make sure he looks the part: the well-groomed hair; the well-cut suede jacket, with matching suede "sailing"-type hat; the silk shirt, opened to the navel; the St Christopher medallion. He firmly believes he is irresistible. He is a bit of a big head. He loves to be the centre of attention. His whole outlook is geared to this end: the charm and the chat. He is a smart lad, too, not short of a few bob. He hit on the idea of running flea markets in church halls and renting out the stalls to traders who were finding the increasing rent and rates on their shops more than a minor problem. It has been a huge success. His work gives him a lot of free time which he spends doing what he thinks he is best at—being the great lover. He is married, but it does not seem to inhibit him. In fact, it acts as a good get-out if things look like becoming too serious*

>(*Surprised*) You're early.

He sweeps through the door. She closes it behind him, and as she turns he engulfs her in his arms

Alan I knew you couldn't wait.

She smiles at his approach

Maggie (*playing the innocent child*) I've been quivering at the knees all morning.
Alan I'll put you out of your misery—let's go to bed.

Maggie pushes away from him

Maggie How very romantic.
Alan There's plenty of time for that—after!

Smiling still, she moves down into the living-room. He follows her, taking off his suede "sailing"-type hat and tossing it on to a chair

Maggie Why didn't you use the key?

He takes it out of his pocket and hands it to her

Alan It doesn't fit.

She takes it and gives it a cursory glance

Maggie Funny ... (*She slips it into a small pocket on her dress without another thought*) D'you want a drink?
Alan At this time in the morning? No, and I don't want you to have one either.

Act I, Scene 1

She gives him a quizzical look

    I don't want anything to dull your senses.

Maggie (*highly amused*) I'm really going to experience something special, am I?

Alan I've never had any complaints.

She goes to the bar

Maggie (*tongue in cheek*) Well, despite the fact that I might miss the opportunity of experiencing heaven on earth, I'm going to have a drink. Are you going to join me—or are you afraid your performance might suffer?

Alan reacts sharply. He has not been expecting this kind of reaction. He does not much like the needle going in

Alan (*sharply*) Vodka! With fresh orange juice.
Maggie Need to keep up your vitamin intake?
Alan Stop getting at me!
Maggie Oh, dear. I didn't realize you were so touchy. I haven't got fresh orange. Bottle all right?

He nods. She makes the drinks and hands one to him

Alan Have to be, won't it.
Maggie Cheers.

He raises his glass and is about to take a sip

    It's laced with Spanish Fly.

This makes him stop momentarily and look at the drink in his hand. Then he realizes, smiles, and drinks

    D'you really think you're going to be enough for me, Alan?
Alan (*angrily*) More than enough ...
Maggie Is that the best you can manage?
Alan What do you expect me to do—beat you?
Maggie Why not?

This also stops him in his tracks: it is not the reception he had been expecting

Maggie I like my men—aggressive.
Alan Oh, come off it, Maggie—this isn't you.
Maggie I see. You've weighed me up, have you? Know exactly what I want and need?
Alan I don't understand. I'm confused.
Maggie Your trouble is that you see every woman as a poor little under-sexed housewife, longing for you to happen along and re-awaken her desires. Well, we're not all like that.
Alan (*unsure of himself*) But, I've watched you. At parties. I've seen how you react when couples pair off and go into bedrooms.
Maggie They disgust me!

Alan (*his confidence returning*) There you are then. So, what's all this about?
Maggie People who flaunt their sexuality in public—are usually pathetic when it comes down to it—if you get my meaning.
Alan You see me that way?
Maggie Partly . . .

He bangs the drink down on the counter

Alan Then what am I doing here?
Maggie You're here because you want me—and because I want you. And because underneath your *obvious* exterior—you've got something. Something different. You don't know how to use it though.

He is a little flattered, and even more curious

You could be good. Very, very good.
Alan (*worried*) No, no—this doesn't ring true . . .
Maggie Go now and you'll never know what you've missed—but you'll always wonder . . .
Alan Are you having me on?

She sits herself down on the Chesterfield and looks up at him—challenging

Maggie I'm trying to open your mind.

She pats the seat beside her. Still more than a little confused, he sits next to her

I know that deep inside you there's a need for change. Quality—not quantity. Why else would you run around this estate testing every Slumberland mattress you can get your back on?
Alan (*laughing and relaxing a little*) Yeah—I do get around.
Maggie I did, too.
Alan (*totally surprised*) You?
Maggie Oh, I don't publicize my—activities. But, after years of marriage—I needed change. I wanted to be in love again—and drunk with it. Christ. When did you last experience that?

There is a moment's pause

Alan I get by . . .
Maggie (*sitting up*) Get by—just get by? Is that all you want? Is it enough?
Alan (*cautiously*) What about Don? Where does he fit in to all this? I don't see him playing this kind of scene.
Maggie Of course you don't. And he doesn't. Don is the type of man who believes a good screw is something with a nut on the end of it and belongs on an Alfa Romeo.
Alan In that case, why do you stay with him?

Maggie is quick to react, realizing he is trying to catch her out

Maggie Because I love him.
Alan Women who love their husbands don't usually do this sort of thing.

Act I, Scene 1 15

Maggie Do you really believe that every married woman you have been with doesn't love her husband?

Alan has not got an answer

Alan Well—they can't, can they?
Maggie Love has nothing to do with sex. They go with you because their husbands can't give them what they need.
Alan (*flattered*) And you think I can give you what you need?
Maggie With a little help . . .
Alan (*relaxing again*) Poor old Don. What he doesn't know won't hurt him, I suppose.
Maggie I tell him the truth whenever possible.

Alan sits up sharply

Alan You mean, you actually *tell* him?
Maggie Why not? He doesn't believe it. I made a special point of telling him about you coming here today.
Alan You *told* him?
Maggie It's the best way.
Alan But, he's my friend . . .
Maggie He thinks you're his friend, too.
Alan Stone me—you've got a cheek. Fancy telling him.
Maggie It's all part of it. Part of the thrill. You should try telling your wife . . .
Alan Marion. The last thing she wants to hear is the truth!
Maggie You're a good liar, are you?
Alan I've told a few whoppers in my time.
Maggie Oh?
Alan How can you be sure Don hasn't spun you a few good yarns?

There is just a flicker of concern in her eyes

I mean, if you can get up to all sorts of tricks. Perhaps he can, too. He's a quiet one, that Don. It's the quiet ones you've got to watch. I mean, what's he getting up to in Cologne. It's a pretty lively city so I'm told.
Maggie (*relaxing*) I know exactly what he's getting up to. He'll be dashing round taking snaps of cathedrals—bridges—statues . . .
Alan (*laughing*) Yes, he likes it more than golf, doesn't he?
Maggie He likes it more than anything.

He takes this as an invitation and slips his arms around her

Alan What's this "something special" you've got in store for me?

She plays up to him a little, running her free hand through his hair and giving him a gentle peck on the lips, before pulling away from him and getting to her feet

Maggie Have you got a favourite fantasy?

There is a moment's pause

Alan I sometimes have this wild dream about being a milkman with nothing on except a blue striped apron, a pair of wellies and a hat. And a tattoo proclaiming: "Drinka Pinta Milka Day" on my bum.

She laughs

(*Sighing*) That's a relief. It's the first time I've made you laugh.
Maggie What do you know about the Borgias? Or Louis the Fifteenth and the French Court?
Alan (*clearly not knowing much*) Well—they were all lads, weren't they?
Maggie They call this the permissive society, but compared to what *they* had to offer it's like having afternoon tea with Mary Whitehouse. Louis the Fifteenth used to play chess using naked men, women and children. They wore specially designed hats to symbolize each chess piece. Believe me. Checkmate really stood for something.

Alan shudders

Alan (*interested now*) Go on.
Maggie D'you know what my current fantasy is, Alan? I want to be taken by a criminal—no, a mad man—from an asylum.
Alan You're not serious, are you?
Maggie I'm serious, love. And, in our case it would need to be someone who'd escaped from Broadmoor say. Someone who'll stop at nothing to get his hands on a woman. That's you, isn't it, Alan?
Alan Well—in a way. Except for the Broadmoor bit . . .
Maggie But, it's a role you could fit into rather easily, isn't it?
Alan Well—if I put my mind to it . . .
Maggie Fine. Well, all you've got to do is think what a man like this would do once he'd broken out. I mean, would he be in a frenzy? A man who has never given a damn for any woman's feelings. All he's ever cared about is his own gratification. He's probably even murdered . . .

Alan is beginning to look and feel very uneasy, but she puts her arms round his neck and grips him

That's you, love—isn't it?
Alan (*uncomfortably*) Well—if that's what you want me to be . . .
Maggie Yes, it's you—isn't it? (*She kisses him passionately, playing him like a fish. All the things she says about him being a sex maniac and only interested in his own gratification and not interested in a woman's feelings, she means. This is how she sees him. She has merely placed her picture of him in a fantasy situation so that he will not recognize himself. She breaks away from him*) Alan, it's going to be great. Are you willing to give it a try?
Alan (*hesitantly*) Well . . .
Maggie Perhaps you're not up to it?
Alan I'm up to anything—anything! If that's what you want.

She turns from him and smiles—a smile of great satisfaction

Maggie I knew I could *rely* on you. (*In fact, she means he is predictable*)

Act I, Scene 1

Alan What have I let myself in for?
Maggie Me! That's what you want?

A moment, as he takes her in

Alan Oh, yes—I want you . . .
Maggie I know. You can't resist, can you?

She gets up from the Chesterfield and goes to the kitchen door. She exits to the kitchen and a moment later returns with a suitcase. She moves back to him with the case and places it on the Chesterfield before opening it

I think there's everything here that we need.

He peers into the suitcase

Alan How d'you manage to keep this from Don?
Maggie I simply leave it lying around. If I made a point of hiding it—then he'd get curious. But, left under his nose—he never notices; and even if he had I would simply have said it was to do with the Drama Society. (*She takes out an arrowed prison jacket*) Here. Put this on.

He takes it from her and holds it up to get a better look at it

Alan I'll look daft . . .
Maggie You're meant to be. (*She laughs*) In the sense that you're a maniac, of course. Put it on.
Alan Well . . .
Maggie It won't be for long.

He takes her meaning and takes off his own jacket, putting it on the Chesterfield. He then puts on the prison jacket and buttons it up. Having done this it seems to get him in the mood. He waltzes around like a fashion model showing himself off

Alan How do I look?
Maggie Very fetching. (*She takes out a pair of arrowed trousers and throws them to him*) These may be a little on the large side.

He takes them and looks at them

Alan We could both get into these.
Maggie Perhaps we will.

He slips out of his own trousers and puts on the prison pair

Alan Well, here I am. Ready for action. Are you?
Maggie I will be when I get into my outfit.
Alan I thought the idea was that I rushed in and ravished you just as you are?
Maggie Not me. I've got to change my character. Make myself more representative of the person you'll be raping.
Alan I'll find the answer to this in a minute—I know I will.
Maggie Yes, you will. But, it's all very simple. You see, I have to be the epitome of innocent womanhood. The kind of woman you take advantage of . . .

Alan I take advantage of?
Maggie (*giving him a handbag*) In the fantasy, of course. (*She actually means this is what he does in reality*) I'm going to become the kind of innocent, unsuspecting person who is always so vulnerable to sexual approaches . . . (*She opens the handbag he is holding so that the mirror on the inside flap is facing her*)

He watches, fascinated, as she takes out a tin of cold cream, puts some of it on a tissue and starts to remove her make-up

(*As she wipes*) Yes, a real innocent. Waiting for something and not quite knowing what it is. (*She finishes removing the make-up, takes some hairpins out of the bag, and commences to tie her hair up in a very severe style*)
Alan Don't do that. I shan't fancy you.
Maggie Oh, you will. You're a sex maniac. You fancy anything. Tell you what. I'll get into my outfit in the kitchen after we've sorted you out.
Alan I thought we'd sorted me out.
Maggie Well, for a start—you've got to escape. How can you be an escaped maniac unless you do?
Alan Escape from where?
Maggie Exactly. We need something to represent a prison. Somewhere you can break out of.

He looks around the room rather dubiously

Alan (*despairingly*) Where?
Maggie Oh come on, Alan, love. Don't leave it all to me. Show some enthusiasm. We've both got to get into this. It's got to take us over.

His eyes search the room

Alan (*eventually*) How about this cupboard on the landing?
Maggie (*looking at it*) Yes. Yes. That's not a bad idea. (*She goes to it, apparently taken with the idea*) It could be a sort of solitary confinement cell, couldn't it? If only it was padded . . .

He moves to her

No. No, it's no good.
Alan No?
Maggie We'd have to repair the lock afterwards—it might show.
Alan Yeah. (*He looks around the room again*) How about the kitchen? I could go in there.
Maggie (*shaking her head*) No. I'll be there.
Alan Oh, yes.

Maggie moves from him, looking round the room. It becomes evident that she is trying to lead him towards the landing and the wrought-iron chair. She stands there, looking at it. He joins her

What about upstairs?
Maggie Well—not very original, is it?

Act I, Scene 1

There is a touch of desperation on his face as he looks around, lost for an idea. She continues to look at the landing and the wrought-iron chair, but she makes it seem as though she too is searching for an idea

Alan (*eventually*) That's it! What about the landing?

She turns to look at him in amazement

Maggie The landing?
Alan (*pointing*) In that chair . . . (*He moves to the landing and indicates the banister rails*) Look. It's even got bars . . . (*He moves quickly up to the landing and sits in the wrought-iron chair*) What do you think?
Maggie Well . . .
Alan It's perfect. Find something to strap me in—and with the bars—well, like you were saying—you know, about Louis the Fifteenth with his hats that symbolized the chess pieces. (*He slaps the wrought-iron chair*) Well, this is symbolic.

There is a brief moment's pause

Maggie And I was going to throw it out today. It's a great idea. Why didn't I think of it myself?

He beams with self-satisfaction

We just need something to keep you locked in—and you're right—it's perfect. I can see this is going to be wonderful—*you're* going to be wonderful . . .
Alan (*smiling*) I have my moments . . .

Maggie moves back to the suitcase and takes out two pairs of handcuffs. Alan relaxes in the chair. Having got the handcuffs she returns to Alan and clamps the first set on his wrist

(*Standing up in surprise*) What the hell are you doing?

She gently pushes him back down again

Maggie Bondage.
Alan Bondage?

She quickly clamps the second set of handcuffs on his other wrist

Maggie I'm kinkier than a bed spring . . .
Alan You're not going to beat me, are you?

By this time she has clamped the two sets of handcuffs to the arms of the wrought-iron chair.

Maggie Would you like me to?
Alan I don't like pain. (*He pauses for a moment, as he realizes his exact predicament. He tries to pull his wrists free*) I shall be here for hours.
Maggie Oh, I *am* surprised at you. Use your initiative. Think of the ways you usually get out of nasty situations.
Alan (*struggling*) Well, I'll never get out of this.

Maggie I'll leave the key where you can get at it ... (*She places it on the banister rail, then ruffles his hair in a rather rough manner before crossing to the kitchen door*)
Alan But I can't move the chair.
Maggie I know. (*As she exits*) I've screwed it to the floor.

Maggie exits to the kitchen

For a moment Alan sits there perplexed and angry. It is almost possible to see his brain ticking over as he tries to work out a way of getting the key. The chair is too heavy for him to move forward since it is carrying his own weight, and his hands are, of course, handcuffed to the arms. Then it occurs to him that he might very well be able to reach the key with his foot. He tentatively raises his left foot—as the key is on that side—and reaches out with it towards the key. He decides it is just about possible to get it. He gets his shoe off without much difficulty, but his sock presents a problem. Finally he solves it by raising his left foot to his right hand and is then able to pull the sock off. He reaches out with his bare foot to get the key. It is just out of reach

Alan (*shouting*) It's bloody impossible ... (*He decides to make another attempt and this time—with great effort—manages to touch the key, only to knock it off the banister rail. Shouting*) I've knocked it off the rail. Can you hear me?

There is still no reply. A moment passes, then the mosaic shutter which separates the kitchen from the living-room shoots up

Maggie, Jane Abbott, Helen Francis and Liz Thomas are revealed. They are lined up at the breakfast counter, staring at him. Each of them has on a barrister's wig and gown. Jane Abbott is in her early thirties, dark and attractive, highly intelligent; a woman trained as a solicitor but married only eighteen months after taking her first job. She is a hard lady. Liz Thomas is thirty and a bit. She is the original dizzy blonde, a former secretary who was cute enough to marry the boss. She is a very pretty lady but her eyes are weak and this necessitates thickish glasses. She is always aware of them, always taking them off. They do not really spoil her looks but she thinks they do. She is a sweet and uncomplicated person, but not especially bright. In fact, behind her back, she is known as Dizzie Lizzie

Alan stares at them. It does not automatically register

Alan I can't get out ...
All We know.
Alan Well, help me.

Maggie leaves the others and enters the living-room. She goes to Alan, picking up the fallen key which she pockets. She stands there, looking at him, not speaking. He looks very much like the prisoner in the dock with her dressed in her wig and gown. He looks at the others, not comprehending

Alan What's all this about?

Maggie You're on trial.
Alan (*bewildered*) What for?
Maggie Your life.

CURTAIN

SCENE 2

The same. Fifteen minutes later

Helen, Jane and Liz are busily putting the finishing touches to the set which has now become a court room. A transformation has taken place. By using props from the production of a play done by the local dramatic society they have created a tremendous effect. A cut-out dock has been placed around the small landing which juts out into the living-room. The bow-front chest/bar has been similarly treated so that it is now a Judge's Bench. In front of this there is a table and chairs where the Clerk of the Court might sit. And there is also a Witness Box. Spotlights, which were already part of the setting, have been placed so that they help with the atmosphere. The curtains are drawn

Jane is clearly to be the Judge of the proceedings which are about to take place. She wears the regalia of a Justice of the High Court. The red robes and the ermine collar—the Judge's emblem of purity—and looks very attractive. She is moving a high button-backed chair into a central position behind the Bench

Alan Jane—what *is* all this about?
Jane (*looking up*) Maggie has already explained. (*She returns her attention to what she is doing*)
Alan Is it one of your silly games?

Jane looks up again, sharply. There is a flash of bitterness

Jane It's no *game*—let me assure you.
Alan Come off it—it's all over the estate—what you lot have been getting up to.

Jane's face is set hard

Jane You're on trial. I suggest you treat it seriously.

Liz looks across at him from the desk in front of the Bench where she has been laying out pads and pencils and folders, etc.

Liz You're really going to get your come-uppance.
Jane (*admonishing*) Be quiet, Liz!

Liz will not be silenced

Liz And not before time!

At this point, Maggie enters from the kitchen, carrying a brown chemist's bottle

Maggie Thank you, Helen.
Helen Do be careful with it . . .
Maggie (*smiling*) Oh, I will—we wouldn't want anyone to get burned, would we? (*She puts the bottle on the breakfast counter and then goes to the desk in front of the Bench*)
Liz Mr Sexton doesn't think we're serious, Maggie.
Jane I informed him we're—*deadly*—serious.
Maggie That's a good choice of words, Jane.
Helen (*worried*) Shouldn't we tell him why he's on trial?

Maggie turns to face Helen who immediately shrinks a little

Maggie (*coolly*) When this Court is formally convened he'll learn what it's all about. Is that clear?
Alan You seem to have forgotten me.

Maggie turns back to him with a smile

Maggie What makes you think that?
Alan It doesn't seem to have occurred to you that I'm not prepared to take part in this stupidity.

Maggie moves closer to him

Maggie (*icily cool*) You'll be given every opportunity to defend yourself. If you're foolish enough not to—you'll be tried—found guilty—and sentenced. Is that clear?

Maggie's manner is so matter-of-fact, it is chilling. Alan is disconcerted. Helen is clearly worried. Jane, however, is enjoying it.

Alan (*uneasily*) What am I supposed to have done?
Maggie In a few moments charges will be read out.

Maggie turns to Jane, who is putting her gavel and block in place on the Bench

Are you ready, Jane?
Jane Unless you want to use any more of the props.
Alan Ah. I thought I recognized all this gear. It's from that play you did at the Masonic Hall over Easter—isn't it? Well, I must admit, Maggie—it's all very theatrical. On with the show. Let's all have a laugh and a joke.

Maggie keeps her cool

Maggie Very well. We can't force you to change your attitude. But, I don't think you'll find it very funny when sentence is passed.
Alan (*rattled by her attitude*) You're potty. (*To the others*) She's gone daft. Can't you see? She's not responsible for her actions. This'll get you into serious trouble—all of you—you see . . .

They all stare at him with set expressions. He finds it very disconcerting

Jane. Jane, love. You've got all your marbles. Don't let this go any farther . . .

Act I, Scene 2

Jane just stares directly at him—not moving a muscle

Jane—if we ever meant anything to each other ... (*He stops, realizing he has probably made a mistake*)
Jane (*after a moment*) I nearly lost my husband because of you.

There is a pause—tense, worrying. He looks from one to the other for a sign which might indicate that he is getting through to them. It does not come. Clearly, they all have something against him

Alan Oh, I see. I get it now. You're trying to frighten me, aren't you? That's what this is all about—isn't it? (*Pause*) Isn't it?

They remain set as he looks from one to the other

(*laughing loudly*) Fine. You win. You've scared the pants off me. Isn't that what you want to hear? Does that satisfy you? (*There is a moment's pause*) Come on, my lovelies. I'm shit scared. It's worked.

It is very clear how rattled he is, and their continued silence does not help. Maggie breaks the silence

Maggie (*to Alan*) As you know, Jane read Law at Edinburgh before she married Richard. She's agreed to act as Judge and to make sure your trial is conducted in a proper manner.
Alan Maggie—come on—bend a little. I'm suitably impressed.
Maggie (*continuing*) However, I must point out that it will be necessary to call Jane as a witness and, indeed, all of us will be giving evidence. I'm explaining this now so that you have no reason to object later.
Alan (*angrily*) Well, I do *object*! I *object* to this whole bloody business! I *object* to you and your insane ideas! I *object*—vehemently—to being treated like this. I *object*! I *object*! I *object*!

Jane bangs her gavel

Jane Objection overruled.

They all laugh

Maggie (*to Alan*) I hope that is the last emotional outburst you'll make during these proceedings. Now. Liz is going to act as shorthand writer. She will be taking notes which you may refer to at any time. (*To Liz*) I'd like you to take your place.

Liz sits down at the desk and prepares her pads and pencils ready to take copious notes

Helen is going to act as Clerk of the Court.

Maggie goes to the desk in front of the Bench and opens a briefcase which is lying there. She takes out a loose-leaf folder and moves to Helen with it. From the folder she produces a sheet of paper which she hands to Helen

Will you call the Court to order and read out the charge.

Helen takes the sheet of paper and steps forward to a central position. She is clearly a little nervous. Alan is quick to notice this

Alan Helen, you don't want to go through with this, do you?

Helen gives him a thin smile—she is jittery

What will Joe think when he finds out—he will, you know.

Helen looks for support

It won't end there. It'll get back to the Golf Club—he'll do his nut . . .

Helen cracks

Helen Shut up! Tell him to shut up!

Maggie moves to her and rests a reassuring hand on her shoulder

Maggie I promise you Joe won't find out, love.
Alan (*shouting*) I'll tell him!

A moment. Maggie crosses so that she is standing close to him

Maggie (*quietly*) I don't think you will. (*She consults her notes*)
Jane I must *warn* you—in the strongest possible terms—that this Court will not be held in contempt. You will be well advised to conduct yourself in a responsible manner. (*To Helen*) Clerk—will you please call the Court to order and read the charge.

Helen casts a quick glance at Alan, who is beginning to despair

Helen This Court is now in session. (*Pause*) Alan Edward Sexton. You are hereby charged with the murder of Rosemary Mancini.

Alan is astounded

Alan Murder? *Murder?*
Helen (*continuing*) In that on the twenty-third day of June this year, you knowingly and wilfully allowed the said Rosemary Mancini to die when it was within your power to save her life. How do you plead?

Alan shakes his head in disbelief

Alan We may as well pack it in now. This is crazy. I don't know anything about Rosemary's death. Nothing at all.
Maggie How do you plead?

Alan's head jerks round to face Maggie

Alan Not *bleeding* guilty—you stupid cow!

Jane thumps the block with her gavel

Jane Prisoner at the Bar. Foul language is totally unacceptable in this Court! (*She pauses for a moment, then turns to Liz*) Will you please make a note that this is the second time the prisoner has been reprimanded?

Act I, Scene 2

Liz makes a note on her pad

Alan (*in sheer frustration*) I'm going potty. Abso-bloody-lutely-potty!
Jane Are we to understand you're making a plea of insanity?
Alan Yes. You're all insane!
Jane (*turning to Alan*) Look. You can go on as you are—but I want you to think about this. Murder is a very serious charge. It's true you haven't got a defence counsel to advise you—and this has been taken into consideration. But, I want you to understand that a *conviction* in *this* Court carries the death sentence.

There is a stunned silence. Helen's mouth drops open, but she does not interrupt. Alan is astonished

Alan Death sentence . . .?
Jane Let me assure you—none of us is a weak-kneed liberal—we all believe in an eye for an eye.

There is a moment's pause, very awkward and tense. Both Helen and Liz look extremely uncomfortable

Alan (*astounded*) You can't be serious.
Jane You will be well advised to treat this trial as if it was happening in a real Court of Law and defend yourself accordingly.

Maggie looks at Jane and nods. It is a sign which says: "Well done!" She refers to her notes before turning to Alan

Maggie You are charged with the murder of Rosemary Mancini. How do you plead?

Alan looks around at the others. Their faces are set, stern, unyielding. Clearly, he is now a little frightened. He makes a decision to play along with them in the hope of getting out of his predicament at a later stage

Alan (*croaking*) All right. Yes, all right. I'll go along with it. I plead—Not Guilty.
Jane (*to Liz*) Will you enter a plea of Not Guilty in the record?
Liz Oh, yes, Jane. Certainly.
Jane And will you, *please*, refer to me as your Honour in future?
Liz Sorry, Jane . . . (*Her hand goes up to her mouth*)
Jane Try to remember you have a very responsible position.
Liz Yes, Jane—I mean—your Honour.

Alan laughs as Liz looks sheepish

Alan She's not known as Dizzie Lizzie for nothing, is she? (*He regrets it even as he says it: another mistake—another enemy*)
Liz (*hurt and angry*) You won't think I'm so dizzy when I tell the Court what I know about you and Rosemary.
Maggie (*interrupting*) Save it for the witness box!

Liz looks mildly defiant for a moment, but goes back to her shorthand pad Maggie turns to Jane

Your Honour. On the morning of the twenty-third of June this year, I took some clothes to be sold at the Nearly New Shop in aid of the Mentally Handicapped.

Alan Is this relevant?

Jane (*to Maggie*) The prisoner does have a point, Counsel.

Maggie I think I can show that it's very relevant, your Honour. If I hadn't gone on this particular errand I might never have noticed the one thing which led me to discover Rosemary Mancini's body.

Jane (*nodding*) Proceed.

Maggie Well. Because of this I missed the milkman when he called. I'd forgotten to leave a note out asking for two extra pints—so I had to find him. I drove round the estate and caught him coming out of number nineteen Lock Close—which was, as you all know, the victim's house. Anyway, there were two bottles of milk on the doorstep and a newspaper sticking out through the letter box. It niggled me . . .

Jane Bothered you?

Maggie Yes. You see, I knew she only ordered one pint a day.

Jane She was living alone. Perhaps she just hadn't needed to use her pint from the previous day.

Maggie Yes, that would explain the two bottles being left out—except . . .

Jane Yes?

Maggie Well, if you remember—at that time we were in the middle of a heat-wave. It was up in the eighties. No housewife would leave milk on the doorstep in those circumstances. I mean, even if she hadn't needed it surely she would have taken it in. Put it in the fridge. Then there was the newspaper. It was gone eleven-thirty. I felt—uneasy. That something was wrong . . .

Alan If you were so concerned—why didn't you investigate?

Maggie is unprepared for this. She consults her notes, trying to gather her thoughts

Come on! I want an answer. Why didn't you investigate?

Maggie Your Honour I'd be obliged if you would instruct the prisoner not to interrupt.

Alan Not to interrupt—you don't want me to defend myself do you? What are you afraid of? That I might prove myself innocent?

Maggie Not a chance, your irrelevant question won't do that for you.

Alan How can it be irrelevant to ask why you didn't knock on Rosemary's front door to see if she was all right?

Maggie Your Honour.

Jane The prisoner has a point.

Alan Thank you, thank you very much.

Maggie (*flustered*) All my instincts screamed at me to check.

Alan Well, *why* didn't you?

Maggie (*still flustered*) I—don't know. I wanted to. But, I had things to do at home . . .

Alan (*sarcastically*) You had things to do at home! Great. So, because you felt it was more important to stick Jeyes fluid down the loo—a

Act I, Scene 2

woman *died*. I put it to the Court: If I'm guilty of murder then the Prosecuting Counsel is too!

Maggie (*to Jane*) Your Honour. I believe the prisoner has brought up a very good point that must be examined.

Alan is amazed. Maggie holds the moment as they all look at her

Where does the burden of guilt lie? Whose ultimate responsibility is it when someone decides to take their life? *We* all knew Rosemary. We are all aware of her circumstances. Her problems. And none of us did very much to help her. But, this argument could go on for ever. Was her husband guilty in some way? Or her parents even? And so on . . .

Jane But, there is a difference in the case you are presenting. Right?

Maggie My intention is to prove that the prisoner *deliberately* allowed Mrs Mancini to die.

Alan Balls! I had as much to do with it as you did. *No*—I had even less. I didn't have anything to do with it. I couldn't have. I had no idea she'd taken an overdose . . .

Maggie (*cutting in*) So you say!

Alan But, you—you had the opportunity to do something.

Maggie True! And in the end I *did* do something. I phoned Rosemary.

Jane And what happened?

Maggie slowly turns from her confrontation with Alan to face Jane

Maggie There was no reply.

Alan Then why didn't you go over to the house and see if she was all right?

Liz suddenly becomes a little overwrought

Liz Please—please—go a bit slower. It's years since I did any real shorthand. (*Near to tears*) And I can't—I just can't keep up—it's not my fault—honestly—I'm rusty . . .

Helen moves to Liz and tries to comfort her

Helen No one expects you to work miracles, Liz. (*To Jane*) It's very exacting work, your Honour. We should make allowances.

Jane In the circumstances, the Court asks everyone to make allowances.

Alan (*with undue deliberation*) Why didn't you go over to the house when you got no reply to your telephone call?

Maggie (*after a moment*) The reason I didn't get a reply was because—the phone was engaged.

The significance of this is apparent to all of them—Alan particularly

Jane So you assumed that Mrs Mancini was speaking to someone else on the telephone?

Maggie Yes, your Honour. But, I didn't just leave it at that. I phoned again fifteen minutes later. It was still engaged.

Alan Are you trying to tell us that after fifteen minutes you weren't in any way suspicious?

Maggie That *is* what I'm saying.

Alan It didn't occur to you to think that something might—just might—be wrong?

Maggie (*to Jane*) Your Honour. I would like to call Helen Francis to the witness box.

Jane Helen Francis.

Helen moves from her position by the Bench and goes to the Witness Box, which she enters. She looks very nervous. Maggie moves to her, smiling

Maggie There's nothing to be afraid of.

Helen I—I'm just a born worrier.

Maggie With your help I intend to establish one point I believe is relevant. It won't take long.

Helen I understand.

Maggie How long did you know the deceased?

Helen Well. Let me see. I met her originally—oh, it must have been all of three years ago.

Maggie When, in fact, she first moved on to the Riverside Park Estate?

Helen That's right.

Maggie What sort of a person was she?

Helen clearly finds this difficult to answer

Helen Well, I—in what way?

Maggie Was she a gregarious person, for instance?

Helen Definitely. I've heard her referred to as "the life and soul of the party" on many occasions.

Maggie Likeable with it?

Helen (*hesitantly*) Lots of people liked her . . .

Maggie And you grew to know her well?

Helen Very well. She became part of everyone's life on the estate.

Maggie So, if you got to know her very well you must have talked to her from time to time at length?

Helen Oh—often. Anyone will tell you—talking to Rosemary Mancini at great length was no problem. Getting away from her was. She used to go on and on and on . . . (*She suddenly realizes what this implies*) Oh, I see . . .

Maggie Thank you. You may step down. (*She turns to Alan*) Unless, of course, the prisoner wishes to question you.

Alan shakes his head, ruefully. Helen moves back to her place beside the Bench

(*To Jane*) Your Honour. I also knew of Mrs Mancini's reputation for being a "chatty person". I've even heard some people suggest that she suffered from verbal diarrhoea. (*Tongue in cheek*) So. When I got the engaged tone fifteen minutes later I assumed she was on a conversational bender which might go on for hours.

Helen I dread to think what her phone bills were like.

Maggie During the day I continued to phone her at regular intervals. I would have returned to her home towards the end of the afternoon had

Act I, Scene 2

not Fate—the good Lord—or however you like to refer to it—not taken a swipe at me with His other hand—temporarily blinding me, so to speak...

Alan Well, you couldn't get through to Rosemary but it appears that "the good Lord" was quite easily able to get through to *you*. He had a direct line almost.

Maggie Yes. I agree.

This causes Alan to raise his eyebrows

Although as you will see it was a crossed line. At around three o'clock I got a phone call. My mother had been taken ill. Seriously. A coronary. I dropped everything and drove to the hospital the other side of Staines. I was there until just after eleven—when she died—(*pause*)—all thoughts of Rosemary Mancini disappeared from my mind.

Jane Understandable.

Liz (*removing her glasses*) Oh, I agree. I remember it well because I was the one who got hold of Maggie's—sorry, Counsel's—husband. It wasn't easy though. I kept trying his office but he wasn't there. It was about eight o'clock before I got him—I think——

Jane (*interrupting her*) Thank you. Will you make a note of it.

Liz starts to do this but can not find her glasses. They have been accidentally pushed to the far side of the table

Jane What's wrong?

Liz I can't find my glasses...

Jane They're by your left elbow.

Liz finds her glasses and puts them on

Why don't you wear contact lenses?

Liz I used to but, Bill kept coming up behind me and surprising me.

Helen Surprising you?

Liz *Goosing* me. And the contact lenses kept popping out. After I lost two pairs he refused to buy me any more. He said fifty pounds a touch-up was too expensive for a cheap thrill—even for him. (*She takes up her shorthand pad. To Jane*) Bill was home late that evening. too. D'you want me to make a note of that as well?

Jane (*long suffering*) If it pleases you...

Liz Well, that's why I remember it so clearly.

Jane Then make a note of it.

Alan She's good for a laugh, isn't she?

Liz (*swiping back*) Just wait till we've finished with you!

Alan Oh, I've already been found guilty, have I?

Liz There won't be a woman around here who'll want to look at you!

Jane bangs her gavel

Alan I'd like to know exactly what you mean by that remark.

Helen (*worried*) What is Liz on about?

Helen casts a glance at Maggie as Jane bangs her gavel

Jane Order! Order!

Alan It sounds as though something's been planned for me—that I'm already guilty no matter what . . .

Liz I don't mean anything—honestly. Only that everyone will know what sort of a man he really is—that's all.

Jane I will not stand for another emotional outburst like this. (*To Alan*) And if it becomes necessary to silence you by some physical means I will not hesitate to order it! Is that understood?

Alan You really hate me, don't you?

Jane Confine your comments to the matter in hand! Now this trial will proceed in an orderly fashion. There will be no more interruptions. (*To Maggie*) Counsel.

Maggie Before I continue I'd like to set the prisoner's mind at rest. There is nothing "planned". Nor has he been found guilty—yet! If he is it will be up to the Court to decide his—punishment—whatever that may be. (*She checks her notes for a moment or two before continuing*)

Alan cannot help noticing that Jane is giving him a hard look

When I returned from the hospital with Don I was in no fit state to think of anything except my own grief. We cabled my brother in Canada and at about six a.m. he phoned. After I'd spoken to him the business of Rosemary Mancini came flooding back. Don told me to forget it. But—I couldn't forget it—couldn't put it out of my mind—for some unknown reason Rosemary Mancini kept creeping back into my thoughts . . .

Alan (*sarcastically*) A premonition?

Maggie Possibly . . .

Alan The good Lord was pulling your chain again, eh?

Jane thumps the block with her gavel. Alan responds quickly

I'm sorry, your Honour. It was a very facetious remark.

Maggie When Don left for the office I phoned again. It was still engaged.

Alan Did you continue to ignore it?

Maggie It could have been left off the hook.

Alan It was—*remember*? And anyone with a modicum of commonsense would have realized that something was wrong. To all intents and purposes the phone had been engaged for twenty-four hours. *Twenty-four hours!* If she was still talking after all that time, she wasn't only suffering from verbal diarrhoea. Someone had given her an overdose of Syrup of Figs. And any *normal* person would have done something about it.

Maggie (*after a moment*) I did. I got in touch with Don and told him I was going to call round there. He was against it. Insisting it was none of our business . . .

Alan Doesn't that make him guilty, too?

Maggie Yes!

Alan is surprised by this

Act I, Scene 2

He just didn't want to get involved. However, I decided I *would* go round to Rosemary's. I rang the bell. There was no reply. So I walked right round the house looking through the windows. It seemed empty. So, I broke in.

Jane We all know what happened when you went into the house. Would you rather leave it as said, since it's obviously distressing?

Maggie turns to Jane

Maggie No.

Jane As you wish.

Maggie (*after a moment*) I got into the house by slipping the window latch with a pair of garden scissors I found in the shed. I went upstairs. As you know, the master bedroom is along the landing to the front of the house. It was all I could do to drag myself along that landing. Outside the door—I froze . . . (*This is clearly having quite an effect on Maggie. She is trembling. For a brief moment she is unable to control it, then she continues*) Eventually, I opened the door—then stepped inside. Rosemary was lying on the floor by the bed—naked. Photographs were strewn all over the bed. *Mostly*—of her children. There was a half-empty bottle of Scotch. A chemist's bottle—for pills. It was empty . . . (*She looks around at them*)

Helen drops her head—she does not want to see the sadness in Maggie's eyes. Suddenly, Maggie becomes animated. She moves around in quick darts from one to the other as she explains what happened

But, the significant thing is that the telephone was clasped in her hand—her fingers gripped so tightly round it they'd gone almost translucent. I realized in an instant what had happened. (*She continues to move from one to the other, forcing them to relive it with her*) D'you remember Marilyn Monroe?

Liz Oh yes, she committed suicide, didn't she.

Maggie Yes and she tried to phone someone for help. Some *unknown* person—who got away with it. You see, she wanted to live just as desperately as Rosemary . . .

Maggie stops in mid-flow. The others are now caught up in it

I shall never forget her face—it said everything. Two things could have happened. Firstly, she tried to phone someone and couldn't get through. Secondly, she did get through. And the person she got through to chose to ignore her. (*She spins round to face Alan as she says this*) Why? Again there are two possibilities. Either the person she got through to thought perhaps she was blackmailing him in some way and that it was a try on—that she hadn't, in fact, taken a fatal overdose. Or—and this is the more likely theory as you will see later—it was easier to allow her to die.

Alan Why can't you be more specific. These suggestions—these allusions—they're meaningless feminine emotionalism . . .

Maggie Meaningless feminine emotionalism—yes—that typifies you—

the masculine arrogance . . . (*She turns slowly away from him, disgust on her face, to address herself to the others*) Because she was a divorcee every man on the estate firmly believed she was *desperate* to jump into bed with him. But—let's suppose she fell for a *real rogue*. Someone with a smooth line in patter. And she believed all his little white lies. His promises to leave his wife and go with her. Until she threatened to tell his wife the truth—or tried by some other desperate means to get him to make up his mind—like attempting suicide. But, if it went wrong—if it went too far—and she sought help—from her reluctant lover . . . Well, you can see what I'm getting at.

Alan (*vehemently*) You can't prove a word of this!

Maggie turns from Alan and moves to address Jane and the others

Maggie The facts are—Rosemary Mancini did have a lover—she did decide to take her life. She did pull back from the brink and try to get help. And, furthermore, we do know—because it was revealed in a post mortem—that she was four months pregnant. What needs to be answered is—who was the man with whom she was having an affair? Who was the father of the baby she was expecting? Who was the person who hung up on her? (*She turns again and moves slowly to face Alan. She stands directly in front of him and waits a moment*) I intend to prove that Rosemary Mancini phoned you. And that you hung up on her. Knowing that by so doing, she would die.

Before Alan can get a chance to refute this accusation the front door opens

Don Parkes enters

They all react—shocked

(*Shocked*) Don!

It is as if Don does not immediately notice what is going on. He probably does, but it does not quite register

Don I couldn't find a phone box that worked—bloody vandals—I got all the way out to the airport—with time to spare—decided to check everything and discovered I'd left the damn contract behind—it wasn't in the folder—I could swear . . . (*He trails off as it all registers; and he looks around, taking everything in—Alan in the chair, Jane behind the Bench, and Liz and Helen*)

Don Maggie—what's going on?

Alan Your missus and her mates have put me on trial.

Don looks at him, as though he is not listening, and moves down the landing stairs into the living-room to face Maggie

Don Maggie?

Alan D'you know what I'm supposed to have done?

Don does not turn to look at him

They say I murdered Rosemary Mancini. *Murdered*.

Act I, Scene 2

Don I want to hear from you, Maggie.
Maggie I'm doing what should have been done. They gave her seven minutes, remember. Seven minutes for an inquest. Well, I'm going to put that right. Don't try to stop me.
Alan Don, for Christ's sake help me get these handcuffs off—they're cutting into my wrists.

Don half turns to him

Don Give me a minute. I want to get to the bottom of this.
Alan I'm sorry to say this, Don—but your missus is a nutcase. She needs help—and so do I. Get me out of this.
Don (*irritated*) Look—stop wittering, Alan. I'll deal with you in a minute. (*He turns back to Maggie*) So you don't think the police investigation or the inquest went far enough. Is that right?

Maggie watches him suspiciously. He is being too understanding for her liking

There's no need to be afraid of me, love. I just want to understand your motives.

There is a moment's pause

Maggie They didn't investigate. They didn't want to know what was behind her so-called suicide. "An overdose of barbiturates while the balance of her mind was disturbed." Q.E.D. She had no-one to fight for her—no-one who cared—no man of her own. It was nice, easy and very convenient to sweep it all under the nearest piece of Wilton. But, *I* care—*we* care. Some people's lives can't be saved. But, she died needlessly . . .

There is a moment's pause as Don weighs up the situation

Don (*to the others*) The rest of you feel the same way? (*He looks from one to the other*) You believe this is the right way to settle it? Jane?
Jane There were a lot of questions left unanswered. We can supply some of the answers and we're pretty sure *he* can supply the rest.
Don But . . .
Jane There'll be no peace on this estate until this is cleared up.
Don So you allowed Maggie to go through with this?
Jane Do you really believe that Maggie could convince all three of us to go along with this if we weren't sure in our own minds that something smelled pretty rotten?
Don All right—I accept that you made up your own minds . . .
Alan What are you talking about? They've been brainwashed—by a nutter . . .

Don spins round angrily

Don (*angrily*) Will you stop insulting my wife!
Alan Well, look at me. Look what she's done to me. At least you could get me out of this.

Don I want to hear from the others! Liz?
Liz I can prove he was with Rosemary on the day she died!
Don Helen. You're keeping what's known these days as a "low profile". I'd like to hear what you've got to say. What's your own opinion?
Alan She hasn't got one of her own . . .
Don It's right what they say about you—your mouth is bigger than an elephant's back passage. Helen?
Helen It's true what Jane says. There is a lot of bad feeling. You men don't really notice it. You go off to work. You've got your golf. The pub on Sundays. But, we're stuck here all the time. There's a lot of rotten things go on here, too. What happened to Rosemary could easily happen to any one of us. There's been times when I've felt pretty desperate. And you men don't care . . .
Don Thank you, Helen. Well. I think there is something to all this.
Alan (*amazed*) You can't be serious.

Don turns to him

Don Yes. I believe you have got a few questions to answer.
Alan Jesus Christ! What a mate. My friend. Some bloody friend!

Don moves slowly to face him

Don I've been thinking. Wondering how they managed to get you here, Alan. If I put my mind to it I can probably come up with a dozen ways of luring you into a trap—and all twelve of them would involve sex in some form or other. (*He pauses*) Think very carefully before you cry Judas.

Alan remains ominously silent. Don turns back to the others

Well, now. It seems that I and the rest of the fellers around here have been pretty insensitive. I must confess, this business with Rosemary left a bad taste in my mouth. Most of us *were* glad when it was over. We were too eager to get it out of the way. And, it hasn't gone, has it? It seems as though there's a demon amongst us—playing havoc with our lives. And I think you're right. It's time we exorcized it.

There is a moment's pause

Maggie Are you trying to say that you're willing to go along with this trial?
Don That's exactly what I'm saying.
Alan You're as potty as she is.
Don I must be. Because I'm about to suggest to this Court that I act as Counsel for the Defence.

There is a moment's pause. They are all a little bewildered by events. Maggie is puzzled by his understanding attitude, to say the least

Maggie What are you up to?
Don For goodness sake, Maggie. What kind of a man do you think I am? It concerns me deeply when four women I respect, find it necessary to

Act I, Scene 2

go to such lengths. Something's pretty rotten here. Questions do need answering. I want this business done—finished with once and for all. Perhaps we can do that here today. I hope so. And the only way I can think of helping is to act for the Defence. Will you accept my offer?

Jane The Court accepts your offer to act for the prisoner.

There is some eye play between Maggie and Don, but neither of them react more than this

Don In that case—I request an adjournment.

This startles the four women

Maggie No!

Don I must consult with my client in private. How else am I going to prepare a defence? Fifteen minutes. That's all I ask. To get his side of the story. I'll pick the rest up as we go along.

Maggie No!

Jane We must allow Defence Counsel's request. It's not fair to expect him to step in at this stage without being briefed.

There is a moment's pause. Jane bangs her gavel

The Court is adjourned for fifteen minutes.

Liz Thank Heavens. I was dying to go to the loo.

Jane moves out from behind the Bench and moves to the kitchen door. Liz and Helen follow

Jane, Liz and Helen exit

Don Why don't you step out into the kitchen to have some coffee, Maggie.

Maggie Just don't try anything.

Maggie turns from him, and exits to the kitchen

Alan You're a bastard. I've got nothing to say to you.

Don For once will you close that gaping orifice of yours and listen. I want you to answer all my questions. Loudly. There must be no gaps in the conversation.

Alan (*puzzled*) Eh? Why—what are you up to?

Don I want you out of here. As quickly, as quietly and with as little fuss as possible. I'll sort the rest out. Just do as you're told. Now. Can you account for your movements on the day Rosemary Mancini took her life?

As Don talks he moves away from Alan to the cupboard under the stairs

Alan (*loudly*) It was so long ago. I mean, June the twenty-third. I don't suppose I could tell you what I was doing last week.

Don (*loudly*) Think! If we can establish an alibi for you then their case falls apart.

Don opens the cupboard door and all the laundry falls out. Frantically he hurls it back in, casting glances over his shoulder at the kitchen, then moves virtually into the cupboard, looking for something

Alan (*loudly*) I remember around that time I took a trip to Norfolk. I was searching for new stock . . .

Don pokes his head out

Don You must keep records. Restaurant bills. They sometimes have dates on them! Anything . . . (*He dives back into the cupboard*)

Alan Well, I send all that sort of stuff to my accountant. It's no good there, is it? I don't know how I can establish an alibi without getting hold of it . . .

Don emerges from the cupboard with a poker and moves quickly to Alan

Don (*quietly*) I knew this would come in useful some time. (*He moves quickly up on to the landing and commences to use the poker as a lever to break the handcuffs away from the arms of the chair. Loudly*) I don't think they'd let me leave here to get your accounts. We'll have to think of some other way. Perhaps they'd let us use the phone . . .

Don is heaving away on the handcuffs with the poker, but suddenly drops the poker as if it has become red hot and springs away from the chair. At the same time, Alan writhes and squirms in the chair, making painful noises. Don is bewildered

The mosaic shutter dividing the kitchen from the living-room shoots up to reveal Maggie

Don turns sharply. On the breakfast counter is a Variable Mains Dropper. Maggie's hand is on the control dial

Maggie That was just a sample. But, if you try to release him again, I'll turn the current on full blast!

CURTAIN

ACT II

The same. Fifteen minutes later

As the CURTAIN *rises the four women are back in the living-room. Don and Alan have got their heads together and it is obvious that they are preparing the defence. Don has a clipboard and is making copious notes. Jane and Maggie are behind the Judge's Bench. The Variable Mains Dropper is on the Bench and Maggie has put Jane in charge of it. Helen and Liz are in their original places. Jane bangs the gavel*

Jane The Court is waiting to resume. Are you ready?
Maggie Yes. But, I think the Defence should be warned not to try anything—tricky.
Don All right. Maybe I was wrong to try and free Alan, Maggie. But, if I wanted to I could walk out of here right now. Call the police.
Maggie (*after a moment*) Go ahead.

Maggie's casualness bothers Don

Don (*indicating Alan*) What about him?
Maggie We won't harm him . . .

Don hesitates. Maggie smiles

> You won't do anything, because if this gets out it's going to cause a lot of trouble. Police. Publicity. We wouldn't be able to hide from it. I can even see a situation arising where you might be asked to resign your directorship . . .

Maggie pauses. They eye each other warily—old friends—old enemies. They know each other's strengths and weaknesses

> You couldn't take it. I'm not saying I could either. But, you couldn't. And I understand. It's much better to smooth things over amongst ourselves.

For a moment Don considers this. He knows it is the truth. He indicates Alan

Don You didn't have to go that far, surely? Wiring that chair up is madness.
Maggie No, Don—it's *insurance*. It's perfectly safe providing he doesn't try to escape or anything else stupid.
Alan When I get out of here—I won't give a damn who knows about this.
Jane What makes you think you're going to get out of here?

An awkward moment. Jane and Alan glare at each other

Alan Are you threatening me again?

Don (*to Jane, very worried*) What do you mean? Of course, he's going to get out of here ...

Jane worries him. He is afraid of her. The fact that she is in control of the Variable Mains Dropper does not help his fears. She smiles sweetly at him as she strums her fingers rhythmically in the Mains Dropper. Then she laughs

Jane Yes, of course, he is—one way or another.

Jane laughs again. Don is really pent up, but she stops him from interrupting

Don't look so worried, Counsel. We're a long way from reaching a verdict—and anything can happen, can't it?

Don is deeply disturbed. It is clear that he feels he should do something to clarify Alan's position—but what?

It's time we got on with it. (*She bangs her gavel*) This Court is called to order in the trial of The Estate versus Alan Edward Sexton. I call on Counsel for the Prosecution to continue with her evidence. (*To Don*) I assume you are in possession of enough facts. (*To Maggie*) Proceed, Counsel.

Maggie moves to a central position where she can address the Court

Maggie Before the trial was interrupted—I was explaining my intention to prove that Rosemary Mancini phoned the prisoner when she was suffering from the effects of a massive overdose of barbiturates and that he hung up on her, knowing that unless she received immediate medical attention she would die. I would like to call Liz Thomas.

Jane In that case, will the Clerk of the Court take over Shorthand Writer's duties? Elizabeth Thomas.

Liz gets up from the desk and moves into the Witness Box. Helen takes her place and picks up the pencil and pad ready to take notes

Maggie Your name is Elizabeth Thomas and you live at number twenty-four Lock Close?

Liz Yes.

Don A point of order, your Honour. The witness hasn't been sworn in.

There is a moment's pause. Clearly, the women have not considered this

Jane (*not too certain of herself*) Witnesses are honour bound to tell the truth without going through the formality of swearing on the Bible.

Don Honour bound! This isn't the Girl Guides, it's giving witnesses *carte blanche* to tell as many lies as they like.

Maggie Are you suggesting that we're all *liars*?

Don I'm suggesting a person on oath is more likely to tell the truth than one that isn't.

There is a moment's pause. They all feel uneasy about this suggestion of swearing an oath

If you're going to give this trial any validity there must be an attempt at

Act II

observing normal legal procedures. If you want to drag it down to the level of a kangaroo court—then go ahead as you are—in this amateurish fashion.

Jane (*angrily*) Does anyone object to testifying under oath?
Liz But I always tell the truth.
Don Then you won't be afraid to swear on the Bible, will you?
Maggie (*to Jane*) Your Honour. You'll find a Bible in the bookcase behind you just to your right. Could you hand it to the Clerk. And, could you please make it clear to the Defence that the same rules apply to them as to us?

During the following, Jane takes a Bible from the bookcase and hands it to Helen

Alan I don't mind taking the oath. *I*'ve got nothing to hide.
Maggie It applies to you as well, Don.

Don is taken by surprise. He turns to face Maggie

Don Me?
Jane It was agreed earlier that each of us could be called as witness. I'll be *very surprised* if you've got nothing to contribute.

There is a disturbing edge in Jane's tone that bothers Don. They eye each other warily

Don But, I know nothing . . .
Jane (*again with the edge in her voice*) *That* remains to be seen. You knew the deceased. You knew the circumstances in which she died. I would think it highly probable that you have *something* to add that will lead to the truth. And, since you've agreed to take part in this trial you must accept the same rules and conditions as the rest of us.

A moment. It is clear that Jane is getting at him. He is about to react angrily, but changes his mind and merely nods agreement to the proposal

(*To Maggie*) May we continue?
Maggie (*to Helen*) Will you swear the witness in, please?

Helen steps forward with the Bible and crosses to the Witness Box with it. Clearly, she is just as nervous as Liz

Helen (*holding it out*) Place your right hand on the Bible.

Liz reaches out with some reluctance and places her hand on the Bible

And repeat after me. I swear that the evidence I give will be the truth, the whole truth, and nothing but the truth, so help me God.

Jane holds out a restraining hand and Helen looks concerned

Jane Sorry, Helen.
Helen (*nervously*) What . . . ?
Jane If we're going to do it let's do it right. (*To Liz*) Repeat after me. I swear by Almighty God . . .

Liz I swear by Almighty God ...
Jane That the evidence I shall give ...
Liz That the evidence I shall give ...
Jane Will be the truth ...
Liz Will be the truth ...
Jane The whole truth ...
Liz The whole truth ...
Jane And nothing but the truth.
Liz And nothing but the truth.

Helen smiles nervously at Jane

Helen Thank you, Jane.
Jane Your Honour!
Helen Your Honour.
Jane You're welcome!

Helen moves back to the desk and sits down to take up her secretarial duties. Maggie moves closer to the Witness Box and addresses herself to Liz

Maggie We've established that your name is Elizabeth Thomas and that you live at number twenty-*four* Lock Close.
Liz That's right.
Maggie What was your relationship with the deceased?
Liz I was a neighbour. I live practically opposite her house.
Maggie So, you've got a clear view of number nineteen Lock Close?
Liz Oh, yes—very.
Maggie Good. On June the twenty-third this year did you have any particular reason for noticing number nineteen Lock Close?
Liz Yes, I did. I was about to mow the front lawn—my husband never does any gardening and we occasionally get complaints from the neighbours.
Maggie You had a complaint that day?
Liz From number twenty-*six*. I'd been on at Bill for days to do it—but, of course, he always had some excuse—and on the twenty-third, Mary—Mrs Leach from number twenty-six—phoned me ...
Don From next door?
Liz We avoid each other whenever possible.
Don I see.
Liz She asked me to do something about the front lawn before the weeds made their way across to her garden. I was furious and complained bitterly about the mongrel monster of hers called Bitsa burrowing under our fence to do its business on our back lawn—it's very irritating because when the grass is long you can't see where he's been—and sometimes, well—I mean, the children bring it into the house and ...

Don gets up, irritated

Don What possible relevance can this have to the case? Is the location of a dog's lavatory of any importance to the circumstances of Mrs Mancini's death?

Act II

Maggie (*with a wry smile*) If your Honour pleases. It's the *little* things in life which are most significant. They help us to remember the big things—the important things. If you'll allow the witness to continue, you'll see what I mean.

Maggie nods to Liz to continue. Don sits

Liz You see. I don't really remember dates and things all that well ...

Don gets to his feet again

Don Then why do you remember the twenty-third of June this year so clearly?

Liz Because it was my tenth wedding anniversary. And so many things happened on that day. It was like a disaster. There was the Leach's complaining about the lawn. Maggie—sorry Counsel—asked me to try to find out where *you* were to explain what had happened to her mother. It wasn't easy. I kept phoning your office but you weren't there and nobody knew where to find you. Bill was late home from work and had forgotten—he'd actually forgotten our tenth wedding anniversary. June the twenty-third is a day I shall never forget.

Maggie Thank you. We've established—I trust to *everyone*'s satisfaction—that June the twenty-third was something of a red letter day for you. Difficult to forget.

Liz I could hardly cope.

Maggie Despite all that was happening—were you able to mow the lawn?

Liz I got round to it at about four-thirty. I dragged the mower round on to the front lawn—then, as I turned round, I thought: my God, they're filthy!

Maggie (*puzzled*) I'm sorry, I don't understand.

Liz The windows. Bill says it's one of his jobs, but I always end up doing them. So, I did.

Maggie After the lawn?

Liz (*not understanding*) The lawn?

Maggie The one you were mowing.

Liz I didn't.

Jane (*exasperatedly*) But, you've just said you got round to it at about four-thirty!

Liz Yes, I know I said that. But, I didn't actually do it in the end. Well, you've seen my lawn, it's obvious I didn't. What I meant was—I got the mower round to do it—(*she pauses for a moment*)—of course, that's where it is. Hidden under all that grass.

Maggie (*exasperatedly*) All right, all right. So you were cleaning the windows—not mowing the lawn.

Liz No.

Maggie Eh?

Liz Not when I went to get the orange squash.

Maggie (*in despair*) What orange squash? What's it got to do with this?

Liz Well, you wanted to know about it!

Maggie You've never mentioned it to me before!

Liz Why should I? You've never asked me. I was thirsty. Cleaning the windows. I went to get myself some. And when I came back I saw someone going into Rosemary's house.
Maggie (*with a sigh of relief*) Ah. Did you recognize this person?
Liz Oh, yes. (*Turning to Alan*) It was him. Alan. The prisoner.
Maggie How can you be sure?
Liz Well. His clothes. The way he walks. I stood there looking at him. That swagger he has—cocky. Shirt unbuttoned to his navel. And that hat—that silly little hat he thinks he looks so good in. There was no mistaking him.
Maggie How did he get into the house?
Liz How d'you mean?
Maggie Did someone let him in—open the door for him? Or did he let himself in?
Liz He let himself in—he had a key.
Maggie I see. Were you surprised to see him go in there?
Liz Yes and no. Well, I know about the prisoner's reputation. But, I didn't know he was having an affair with Rosemary at that time.
Don (*rising*) Your Honour. How can the witness possibly conclude that the prisoner was having an affair with the deceased simply because she *thinks* she saw him going into the house?
Liz I *did* see him.
Don Did you?
Jane (*to Liz*) You must confine your evidence to what you actually saw. It's not possible to assume they were having an affair simply because you saw the prisoner entering the house.
Maggie Why else would he have a key?
Don I fail to see how the possession of a key can establish anything. (*He sits*)
Jane I agree with the Defence. The handing over of this key does not of itself establish a sexual relationship. Proceed.
Maggie (*to Liz*) You saw the prisoner enter the house. Did you see him leave?
Liz No, I didn't. I finished the windows. The kids were yelling for their tea. I did occasionally glance across at number nineteen. I didn't see him leave. But, I did see him returning later that evening.
Maggie About what time would this be?
Liz Seven o'clock.
Maggie What makes you so sure?
Liz My husband still hadn't come home from the office. I was looking out of the window watching for him when I saw the prisoner—and you won't believe what happened.
Maggie Tell us.
Liz He walked in and said: "Get off your big, fat arse you lazy moo, I want my dinner."
Maggie (*furiously*) You clearly don't mean the prisoner?
Liz Don't be silly. Of course not. Bill. My husband. And on our wedding anniversary, too. Well—the least I expected was a pat on the bottom and a promise of better things to come later.

Act II

Maggie (*barely controlling herself*) Just tell us how the prisoner comes into it!
Liz I already have. I was looking out of the window and I saw him go back into number nineteen! That's how I'm so sure of the time ...
Maggie (*giving in*) Yes, of course ...
Liz (*indignantly*) Our grandfather struck seven.
Maggie I see ...

There is a moment's pause

(*Tentatively*) Did you see him leave this time?
Liz No. But, I couldn't help wondering what was going on. Having seen him twice let himself in.
Maggie Thank you. (*She turns to Don*) Your witness.

Don consults his notes briefly, then moves to Liz in the Witness Box

Don You claim to have seen the prisoner enter the deceased's house on two separate occasions that day?
Liz Yes. I did.
Don Living opposite it would be difficult *not* to notice things going on there?
Liz Well—I'm not a nosey person, you know.
Don I wasn't suggesting you were. Did you notice the milk on the doorstep and the newspapers sticking through the letter box?
Liz (*a little flustered*) I may have.
Don So you did notice them?

A moment, while Liz thinks about this

Liz I—I can't remember ...
Don But, you said you remember everything so clearly on that particular day. I'm talking about June the twenty-third. Your tenth wedding anniversary. A red letter day. A day you'll never forget ...
Liz (*flustered*) Yes, but not all the *tiny* details ...
Don And yet you *clearly* saw the prisoner enter the house on two separate occasions. You knew it was him because of his walk—his hat—his shirt unbuttoned down to his navel. You saw—and remembered—all these *tiny* details clearly enough.
Liz Well—yes—I did ...
Don You sound a little doubtful. But, there was no mistaking him, you said.
Liz (*very flustered*) Did I ...?
Don Only a few moments ago. Surely you remember?
Liz Well, I must have—if you say so.
Don I do. I do indeed. Why have you never come forward with this information before?
Liz I don't understand ... (*She looks to Maggie for help*)
Maggie Your Honour—the witnesses's motives for withholding this evidence previously has nothing to do with this trial.
Don I hope to prove it has, your Honour.

Jane Witness must answer the question.

It almost seems that Jane is enjoying Liz's predicament. There is a faint smile on her face

Liz Well, it wasn't my fault. I would have gone to the police, but Bill stopped me.
Don Why?
Liz (*very flustered*) Well—he said he didn't want to get involved ...
Don Perhaps we could take you over the conversation you had with him about it. I mean, you actually said to him: I want to go—or I think I ought to go to the police about what I saw?
Liz (*after a moment*) Something like that ...
Don But not exactly?
Liz No.
Don Then what?
Liz Well—after they found Rosemary—I told Bill what I saw ...
Don Yes?
Liz Well, he laughed at first—and made a few obscene remarks about Alan—but, when I told him I thought I should go to the police—he was furious. He kept saying they'd tear me to pieces in a witness box—I was so *thick*—he said I couldn't be sure it was Alan ...
Alan He said you couldn't be sure ...
Liz (*a little frantically*) But, I was—I was. I *knew* it was Alan going into Rosemary's house. You see, he always insists on being given a key to let himself in. He says there's less chance of being spotted by some busybody.
Don I see. (*He turns from her to consult his notes when it suddenly dawns on him. He swings round to confront her again*) How do you know he always insists on being given a key to let himself in?

Liz is totally unprepared for this. Her face reveals all. For a moment she is speechless

(*Relishing the moment*) Did you hear the question?
Liz (*biting her lip*) Yes ...
Don (*his voice is hard*) Were you having an affair with the prisoner?

Maggie springs to her feet

Maggie Your Honour. The witness's relationship with the prisoner is not in question and has nothing to do with this case.
Jane (*in a hard, bitter tone*) I think it has everything to do with it! (*To Liz*) Answer the question.

There is a moment's pause

Alan I'll answer it for her! We *didn't* have an affair. Because she's trouble, that one! All she wanted was revenge ...

Don spins round to face him, so angry he could throttle him

Don You fool! You damned fool!

Act II

Liz (*bitterly*) I wouldn't let him lie next to me if he was ten times as good as he thinks he is. He wanted to. Oh, yes—tried every trick in the book. Picked me up in the High Street—took me to lunch.
Alan You lying bitch!

Clearly, a slanging match is about to begin

Jane (*to Don*) Control him or I'll have him gagged!
Alan (*determined that nothing is going to stop him*) You don't want to hear the truth. None of you!
Liz Oh!
Alan *She* picked me up. We went for a few drinks. Naturally I was flattered—who wouldn't be—having a bird throw herself at you? But then she had one gin too many and it all came tumbling out. Her old man was having it off with Allison Phillips . . .
Liz (*taking off her spectacles*) It's a lie! A wicked lie! My Bill going with a nineteen-year-old kid. It's ridiculous! I've got more to offer him than that flat-chested little miss will ever have. (*She turns to Jane*) That's how he tried to get me to go to bed with him. By telling me Bill was going with Allison . . .
Alan You're lying, Liz—lying through your back teeth!
Liz That's when he asked me for the key . . .
Alan Yes, I did. But, I never damn well used it. Because I've got a nose that can smell trouble . . .
Liz He thought I'd believe his rotten, wicked story about Bill—and—and do what he wanted me to—my Bill has never been unfaithful to me. Never, never, never!

Jane bangs her gavel several times. There is silence

Jane (*in a hard voice*) Will Counsel rise!

Maggie and Don move cautiously to her

I will not have these proceedings turned into a slanging match. This case will be conducted in an orderly and *dignified* manner. Is that understood?
Don I'm sorry. I apologize for my client's outburst. I was simply trying to establish that the witness's evidence was coloured by her relationship with the prisoner.
Maggie A relationship which on the prisoner's own admission never existed . . .
Don A qualified admission!
Maggie (*to Jane*) Is it any wonder that the witness should get upset by Defence Counsel's heinous suggestions regarding her husband who is not here to defend himself?
Don But, has it not been established that *something* took place between the witness and the prisoner? Clearly, she knew about the key . . .
Maggie Only because the prisoner *tried* to trick her into an illicit relationship!
Don On the other hand. If the prisoner is telling the truth—that Bill Thomas was having an affair—would she not seek revenge in some way?

Maggie That's the whole point. *Is* the prisoner telling the truth?
Don Is the witness?
Liz (*bitterly*) We didn't have any problems—we've always been all right together.
Don (*referring to his notes*) And yet he forgot your wedding anniversary—even called you a lazy moo for not having his meal ready. *And* when you suggested you ought to go to the police to tell them what you knew about Rosemary Mancini's death he was furious. Said you were *thick*. That they'd tear you apart in the witness box. I believe you didn't go to the police because both you and your husband were afraid of what might come out under cross-examination. That your marital problems might get aired in public!
Liz Oh!
Maggie Your Honour! Defence Counsel's suggestions are offensive and distressing.
Jane (*to Don*) I was about to suggest that Defence Counsel moderate his manner.
Don My only intention is to establish—beyond all doubt—that the prisoner did not enter number nineteen Lock Close at all on that day.
Liz (*to Jane*) I want it to go on record that I knew it was Alan Sexton who went into Rosemary's house not because he used her front door key—*but because I actually saw him.*
Don (*after a brief pause*) How long have you been wearing spectacles?

Liz replaces her spectacles

Liz A couple of years or so . . .
Don How did you come to realize that your eyes needed examining?
Liz Well. (*Pause*) We were in the car park. The one down by the river, you know?
Don Yes.
Liz Well, Bill had just got his new Mercedes and was very proud of it. Treated it like a baby, he did. He even slept in it the first night he got it.
Don Please—stick to the point.
Liz Sorry. Well, you see—he wanted a pee. He was desperate. He couldn't even wait to park the car. He told me to do it. (*With a dramatic sigh*) Well, I'm only used to his little Mini.
Don *Please!*
Liz Well. I drove his precious Mercedes straight into the river. I didn't see the edge. I went right over it. I got out, but the car went floating down towards Windsor.

Don's irritation amuses the others

Don (*with a sigh*) And, after all that, would you say that without your glasses your eyesight is very poor?
Liz It's not good . . .
Don Were you wearing them on the twenty-third when you were cleaning the windows or mowing the lawn?

Liz clearly does not recall

Act II

You're not sure?
Liz I must have been—I think ...
Don But, isn't it a habit of yours to take them off when you're not really in need of them?
Liz Well—they're not very flattering, are they?
Don And you're a very pretty lady ...

Liz smiles, pleased

With the Court's indulgence I would like to demonstrate with a little experiment.
Jane (*to Maggie*) Have you any objection?

Maggie is wary

Maggie No—with the proviso that this "little experiment" is relevant.
Jane (*to Don*) Go ahead.
Don Would the witness please step out of the box.

Liz does so, cautiously

(*To Liz*) Will you go over to the kitchen door, please?

Liz moves to the kitchen door

Now. Would you say that the distance from the kitchen door to the front door is about the same as that from your house to Rosemary Mancini's?
Liz No. It's nowhere near.
Don Will you please take your glasses off and face the kitchen door?

Liz does so, but still with caution. She is a little worried

Don't turn round until I tell you.

Don crosses quickly to the front door, picking up Alan's suede hat on the way. As he passes Alan he whispers into his ear. He then proceeds to remove his jacket, put on the hat and undo his shirt to the navel. When this is completed he nods to Alan, who ducks down so that he cannot be seen

Alan (*to Liz*) You can turn round now.

Liz turns round and gasps

Put your glasses back on, Liz.

Liz replaces her spectacles

Liz I thought ...
Don I was the prisoner. You can sit up now, Alan.

Alan sits up. Don puts on his coat and tie

Maggie Your Honour. I really must protest. Counsel's "little experiment" merely underlines the fact that the witness's eyes are poor. A fact that she has already agreed. It in no way establishes that she was not *wearing* her glasses on the day in question.

Don But, it has been established that the witness doesn't remember if she was wearing them at the time. I quote: "I must have been—I think." Doesn't that suggest there was some doubt in her mind?
Maggie But, she clearly *saw* exactly how the prisoner was dressed—down to his shirt being unbuttoned to the navel. Apart from his hat and his swaggering, cocky walk. Doesn't this suggest she *was* wearing her glasses?

Don, having put his jacket back on, comes back into the living-room, returning the hat to its former place

Jane Have either of you any more questions for this witness?
Don (*too confidently*) No. Since I've clearly established an element of doubt in her evidence . . .

Jane bangs her gavel

Jane *That* is for me to decide! And what's more, I don't agree that you have established that particular point to the complete satisfaction of this Court. (*To Maggie*) Counsel?
Maggie (*smiling*) No more questions, your Honour.
Jane (*to Liz*) Witness may stand down.
Maggie Your Honour. If Liz will resume her duties as Shorthand Writer and Helen take over from you, I would like to call you to the witness box.

Jane goes to the Witness Box as Helen takes her place at the Bench, and Liz resumes her duties as Court Secretary. Maggie picks up the Bible from the table and moves to Jane with it

Take the oath, please.

Jane places her hand on the Bible

Jane I swear by Almighty God that the evidence I shall give will be the truth, the whole truth and nothing but the truth.

As Maggie returns the Bible to the desk, Don gets to his feet

Don This just won't do!

Helen looks confused, as do the others

Helen I don't understand. The witness has merely taken the oath.
Don It means nothing for her to swear on the Bible.

A thin smile crosses Jane's face

It's well known on this estate that Jane Abbott is an atheist. Any evidence she gives on oath is meaningless.
Jane It's simple enough. I'll affirm. I know how to.
Maggie Will you please affirm then?
Jane I—Jane Abbott—do solemnly, sincerely and truly declare—and affirm—that the evidence I shall give, will be the truth, the whole truth, and nothing but the truth.

Act II

Maggie Thank you.
Jane Before I give evidence I would like to make a statement to the Court.

Maggie turns to Don

Maggie Have you any objection?
Don (*to Jane*) What's it about?
Jane I want my relationship to the prisoner made clear now. I'm not going to give you the chance to say my evidence is—tinted—later on.

Don shoots a look at Alan—a touch of contempt

Don I see. Carry on.
Jane From August last year to the beginning of February this year I was out of my mind. I must have been. I really believed the prisoner was in love with me. (*She takes a deep breath*) After my third miscarriage I was very depressed. Well. I was an all-round failure. As a wife. A mother . . . I didn't even have a career any more. (*Bitterly*) Richard had insisted I give it up. I started tippling. I'd have a quick one for elevenses . . .
Alan (*interrupting, glaring at Maggie*) Some people I know can't wait for elevenses even!

Don looks from Alan to Maggie. She gives nothing away. Don turns back to Alan and puts his finger up to his lips

Don (*viciously*) Keep it buttoned! (*To Jane*) I'm sorry . . .
Jane By twelve o'clock I was on my third or fourth and getting ready for a wet lunch down at *The Duke*. One lunchtime Alan came into the pub. Bought me a large vodka, then another—and another. Made me laugh—first time for ages. I even planned to leave Richard for him. We were—in quotes "madly in love". We arranged to go away together. I was to meet him at the *Roundhead and Cavalier* near Cirencester where he'd booked a room for us. I got there at seven. At ten o'clock there was a knock on the door. It took only two steps for me to get across that room and open it. (*Pause*) It was my husband Richard. (*A longish pause*) It was a long time before we could work things out between us. You see, I was still nuts about—Don Juan—for ages afterwards.

During the above Alan avoids looking at Jane, but now he looks directly at her

Alan At least it got you off the booze.
Jane Yes. I do have *something* to thank you for.
Maggie Are you ready to continue?
Jane Yes.
Maggie What do you know of the prisoner's relationship with Rosemary Mancini?

There is a moment's pause. Jane puts her hand into the pocket of her robes and brings out a large diary. She holds it up so that it can be clearly seen

Jane This is a complete record of the times he saw her, when and where.

Alan's interest is reawakened

Alan A *record*? I *didn't have* a relationship with her—how can you have a record?
Jane Do you want me to continue?
Maggie Please.
Jane The first date—rather ironically—is February the fourteenth. Valentine's Day. You'll remember you had a party in this very house.
Maggie Clearly.
Jane I didn't want to come because I knew he'd be here. But, Richard insisted. He wanted us to put on a united front.
Don I don't understand. How is this significant to Rosemary Mancini's death?
Jane I'm coming to that. As the evening wore on I noticed he was getting more and more friendly with Rosemary. Naturally, I was jealous. But, I got caught up in conversation and when I looked up, both he and Rosemary were missing.
Maggie Did you look for them?
Jane Yes. When Richard wasn't looking I slipped out through the kitchen and eventually found Rosemary and Alan in the garden shed—making love.
Alan (*shouting*) It was only that once. I swear. There were no other times. It was just—one off...
Maggie Thank you. You've just confirmed at least one of the entries in the witness's diary.

Alan shuts up, realizing that it looks bad

Jane I never came back to the party.

There is a moment's pause. She holds up the diary

But, I couldn't get Alan or Rosemary out of my mind. I don't know why I decided to keep a watch on them—perhaps there was some thought in my mind of revenge at the time—but, I *did* make this record.
Don I'd like to see that diary.

Jane hands the diary to Maggie, who goes and hands it to Don. He browses through it, makes a quick note and hands it back to Maggie, who returns it to Jane

Thank you.
Maggie (*to Jane*) Each entry in this meticulously kept record represents a meeting between the prisoner and the deceased?
Jane From Valentine's Day on. For instance, on February the twenty-first I waited outside Rosemary's house in Lock Close and followed her to the *Red Stag Motel* near Wokingham.
Don Are you saying that despite traffic conditions—and the fact that you probably had to keep your distance—you were still able to stick with her all the way to the *Red Stag*?
Jane Once I saw the direction she was going in, I didn't really have to follow her. You see, I'd been there many times before—with the prisoner. I even knew the chalet they'd be using.

Act II

Maggie But, did you make absolutely sure they were together?
Jane I went along to chalet fourteen and saw them there.
Maggie Now. It isn't necessary to establish other meetings at the *Red Stag* or any other venue—except those which took place at the deceased's home.

Jane opens the diary and quickly flicks through it

Jane They very seldom met at number nineteen Lock Close. But, when they did, the meetings are recorded in here.
Maggie How did the prisoner get into the house?
Jane He had his own key.
Maggie Thank you.
Alan It's a lie! I never had an affair with her. I never met her at the *Red Stag* or anywhere else. Once we had it off. *Once*.

Helen finds the courage to bang the gavel

Helen I'm not used to this—but, I'm sure it can't be right for outbursts like this to occur in Court.
Maggie (*smiling*) You're absolutely right, your Honour. Prisoner and his Counsel realize they've been suitably admonished.
Alan (*angrily*) How do you expect me to sit here listening to this rubbish and remain calm?

Don sighs, then appeals to the women. After a moment's pause Don gathers himself and his thoughts together. He briefly consults his notes, then moves to Jane. Jane gives him a curiously odd smile. She realizes she must keep her wits about her; and he is also aware that he is dealing with a very clever lady

Don Meticulously kept record. That's how the Prosecuting Counsel described your diary. A diary of deceit. Would you say—that it was a very strange sort of record?
Jane In what way?
Don A detailed account of the times your ex-lover jumped into bed with another woman is hardly the sort of record any normal person would keep.
Jane It depends on the person.
Don Exactly! And what sort of a person keeps this kind of record?
Jane One like me.
Don Obviously. There's an old saying ...
Jane (*cutting across*) "Hell hath no fury like a woman scorned"?
Don You agree with it?
Jane Very much so.
Don Are you that sort of woman?
Jane (*smiling*) Without wanting to put too fine a point on it—yes!

There is a moment's pause. Don finds her frankness a little disconcerting

Don You find it amusing, do you?
Jane I find *you* amusing. Why don't you come straight out and ask me if I hate the prisoner?

A moment. Don is worried by her attitude

Don Do you hate him?
Jane Yes. Very much. But there's been no attempt on my part to hide my feelings. I made it clear from the start.
Don Is that why you kept a diary?
Jane How could it be? I had no idea Rosemary Mancini was going to take an overdose—or that he would hang up on her and let her die . . .

There is a moment's pause. Don smiles

Don So *he is* already guilty in your eyes.

Jane bites her lip—a tiny mistake she regrets

Jane I didn't mean that . . .
Don That's what you implied.

Jane does not reply. The looks between them say enough

(*After a brief pause*) May I have another look at your diary?

Jane hands it over to him. He flicks through the diary and finds the page he is looking for

(*Holding the diary up to Jane*) The last entry is on the eighteenth of June this year. The record then comes to a complete and sudden stop. Why?

There is a moment's pause. They eye each other warily

Have you no answer? Or perhaps there isn't one?
Jane Oh, there's an answer.
Don Then, I repeat. Why does it end so abruptly on June the eighteenth?
Jane (*sighing wearily*) Because I went on holiday on the nineteenth.

Liz giggles. Don knows he has been made to look foolish

To Corfu. For three weeks. You can check on it if you like. When I got back Rosemary was dead—so I couldn't continue with it. Could I?

There is a moment's pause. Don is furious

Don You've been very clever.
Jane No, no, no. You've been very stupid. It only makes me look as if I'm clever.

Liz laughs out loud this time, and it is all the others can do to stifle their giggles

Helen Shhh!
Don Well, *I* view this matter very seriously.
Jane So do I. And since you take it so seriously, I believe it was very remiss of you to look only at the first and last entries in my diary. May I suggest that you take a look at the entries for the week ending the seventeenth of April?

Act II

Don is both embarrassed and furious, but he carefully turns the pages of the diary to the week in question

You'll see that the prisoner met the deceased on three separate occasions. Tuesday, Wednesday, Thursday.
Don According to this, he did. (*He smiles. His confidence returning*) Which brings me to my next point.
Jane Oh?
Don That none of these dates, times, places can be corroborated. So it is your word against my client's. I'll even go farther and suggest that they are all figments of your imagination. (*He waves the diary under Jane's nose*)

A moment

Jane But, I have a witness.

Don is again worried, wondering what she is up to

Don A witness?
Jane Yes.
Don Well—can you produce this witness?
Jane Oh, yes. The witness is here.
Don (*very warily*) Then—who is it?

There is a moment's pause

Jane You.
Maggie Don.

Don is astonished, stunned. Everyone turns to look at him. Clearly, he is totally bewildered

Don I—I don't understand . . .
Jane I don't suppose he noticed—since he's apt to give everything only a cursory glance—but, if you check the diary again for the week ending the seventeenth of April, you'll notice that the venue changes from the *Red Stag* to the Links Motel near Watford.

Don looks up from checking the diary. For a moment there is a look of fear in his eyes

Don I—I'm not quite sure what you're getting at . . .
Jane It's only seven months ago. Surely you remember?
Don (*with a dry throat*) Remember?
Jane We bumped into each other there. You were meeting a client for lunch. You said to me: "Isn't it a small world. I've just had to avoid Rosemary Mancini and Alan Sexton, and I've bumped straight into you." You even went on to say: "I don't know what they're up to—best to keep out of their way." Surely you remember? (*There is a look of triumph on her face*)

There is a moment's pause. Don looks at the diary—then at Jane. He composes himself

Don Seven months—but, I do recall the incident now . . .

Alan is unable to control himself any longer

Alan How the hell can you recall something that didn't happen?

Helen bangs the gavel

Helen The prisoner is advised not to interrupt!

Jane Remember I said to you: "If you're seeing a client don't worry about me. I don't mind if you don't buy me a drink." And you didn't. You went off to find your client.

Don Did I do that?

Jane It was very rude of you, I thought at the time. But, that was one of the occasions Rosemary was with her *lover*. I stayed until they left.

Don Well, I'm sorry about that. You see, it was a *prospective* client— from the north. That's why we decided to meet at Watford—the M.1. It was convenient . . .

Jane Very convenient—as it turns out.

Alan is unable to control himself again

Alan I tell you it's impossible—impossible. You must be mistaken . . .

Maggie May I suggest that you stand down now, Jane. To allow Don to take the witness box.

Don (*a little too fast*) Is that necessary? I mean—I agree with the witness. I was at the Links Motel. I suppose it must have been around that period . . .

Jane leaves the Witness Box and goes to the Bench

Maggie I want the witness's statement confirmed on oath. And as you're not absolutely clear in your mind of the dates, perhaps we can confirm that too.

Helen leaves the Bench and returns to her original position. Maggie indicates the Witness Box to Don, and he enters hesitantly. Maggie gets the Bible from the table and moves to him with it

Take the oath.

He places his hand on the Bible

Don I swear by Almighty God, that the evidence I shall give, will be the truth, the whole truth, and nothing but the truth.

Maggie returns the Bible to the desk and turns back to face Don

Maggie I believe the week in question is that ending Sunday the seventeenth of April? Which day of the week did the incident occur?

Don I can't remember.

Maggie turns to Jane

Maggie Can you help, your Honour?

Jane Wednesday, the thirteenth. (*She smiles as she says it*)

Act II

Maggie turns back to Don

Maggie On Wednesday the thirteenth of April were you at the Links Motel near Watford?
Don I was there around that time. I can't pin it down—

He turns to face Jane, who smiles benignly at him

—as definitely as the previous witness.
Maggie Very well. But whilst you were there did you see the prisoner with Mrs Mancini?

There is a tense and awkward pause as Don and Alan look at each other

Don If the previous witness says so, I suppose I did ...
Alan (*shouting*) You couldn't have. I wasn't there. How could you possibly see me?
Don It—was just a fleeting glance. I could have been mistaken.

Don casts a quick glance at Jane, whose face remains expressionless

Maggie But did you not say—(*she checks her notes*)—"Isn't it a small world. I've just had to avoid Alan and Rosemary and I've bumped straight into you"? (*She looks up*) Well?
Don As far as I can remember—yes. Something like that.

Alan is again unable to control himself

Alan You were seeing things. (*With a sudden thought*) Either that or you're lying!

There is a moment as Don and Alan look at each other with daggers drawn. Surprisingly, Jane comes to Don's aid—albeit with a double-edged sword

Jane But, the witness is on oath. (*A small smile crosses her face*)
Maggie (*to Don*) You may stand down.

Don crosses in front of Alan. They eye each other warily. Don is clearly shaken

Don (*shakily*) I'm sorry. But there was an occasion—Jane is right ...
Alan You're lying. You're bloody lying, aren't you?

Jane bangs the gavel to call for order

Don Your Honour. Since my client appears to have lost all confidence in my ability to defend him perhaps it would be better for him to conduct his own defence.
Jane The prisoner is clearly overwrought and emotional. Nothing will be gained by him taking over his own defence. It can only make matters worse.
Alan He's bloody lying!
Jane According to you, we're all lying!

There is a moment's pause. Jane addresses Maggie

Would you like to continue, Counsel?

Maggie I would like to recall Helen Francis.
Jane Helen Francis.

Helen shifts nervously into the Witness Box

Maggie Although you've already given evidence, you haven't taken the oath.

Maggie picks up the Bible and goes to the Witness Box with it. Helen places her hand on it

Helen I swear by Almighty God that the evidence I shall give will be the truth, the whole truth, and nothing but the truth.

Maggie returns the Bible to the table and turns to Helen

Maggie I want you to think back to Sunday, March the twenty-second...
Helen Yes.
Maggie You were at home...
Helen Yes, my husband returned from *The Duke* with the prisoner.

Alan is again unable to control himself

Alan I remember it. I remember it well. You weren't there. *She wasn't there*.

Jane bangs her gavel. There is a moment's pause

Maggie (*to Helen*) Where were you at the time?
Helen Hiding in our bedroom.
Maggie Hiding. So your husband had no idea you were there?
Helen No. And he still doesn't know, I overheard them.

Don turns angrily to Alan

Don Perhaps this will teach you to keep your mouth shut. If you had—this evidence would have counted for nothing. But, you've actually corroborated it yourself!
Jane (*to Don*) I sympathize with your feelings, but this trial must be allowed to continue with...
Don (*interrupting angrily*) Must it! Must it continue. Haven't we all had enough?
Alan Well, I have. Just get me out of here!

Jane indicates the Variable Mains Dropper

Jane If you think for one moment that I'd hesitate to throw the switch...

Don moves quickly to Jane, holding up a restraining hand

Don All right—all right. I'm sorry. I understand how you feel about him. But, we're all on edge. We say things we don't mean. Let's get on with it.

There is a moment's pause

Jane (*to Maggie*) May we continue?

Smiling, Maggie turns her attention back to Helen

Act II

Maggie So your husband had no idea you were in the house?
Helen No. I heard him come in—talking animatedly to someone—so I crept along the landing and listened.
Maggie What was the subject of their conversation?
Helen Abortion.

There is a awkward pause

Maggie Could you explain in a little more detail?
Helen The prisoner was trying to persuade my husband to prescribe something to procure an abortion.
Maggie For anyone in particular?
Helen Rosemary Mancini.
Maggie Thank you. (*To Don*) Your witness.

Don moves to Helen, checking his notes as he crosses

Don You say you were upstairs in the bedroom when your husband came home with the prisoner?
Helen Yes.
Don You moved along the landing and listened at the top of the stairs?
Helen It was difficult to hear what was being said from the bedroom.
Don Could you see them from the top of the stairs?
Helen No. You can't see into the living-room from the very top. These houses are designed that way. Open-plan downstairs—but the upstairs is totally cut off so that too much noise doesn't filter up to the bedrooms—(*a tiny smile*)—or down.
Don So you couldn't see who it actually was with Joe?
Helen Well. Since I know the prisoner reasonably well, and since Joe kept referring to him by his Christian name—and at one stage it got rather heated and caused Joe to say—well, he swore at him and called him "Sexton" on this occasion. So, I think I can safely say it was the prisoner.

There is a moment's pause

Don Did the prisoner at any time suggest that he was responsible for Rosemary Mancini's condition?
Helen (*hesitantly*) Well, it was obvious, wasn't it? Why else would he ask Joe to help him?
Don I didn't ask you for an assumption. I asked if you heard him accept responsibility.
Helen (*after a brief pause*) No ...
Don I see. Well, did he at any time suggest that he was responsible?

There is a moment's pause

Well?
Helen He said he didn't know who it was and he was only trying to help her because she'd asked him. Joe didn't believe him.
Don Why did the prisoner choose to go to your husband for help?
Helen Well—because he's a chemist, I suppose. And I understand from

what I overheard that Rosemary had only just realized she was pregnant. She thought Joe could give her something.

Don Is that the only reason?

Helen (*warily*) I—I don't understand ...

Don Well, let's see if we can help you understand. Why were you—hiding—from your husband?

Helen (*flustered*) Well—he didn't know I was in the house ...

Don Obviously. But, why weren't you supposed to be there?

There is a moment's pause—awkward and tense

Helen (*appearing casual*) We had a stupid row over a phone call he received. It all seems so silly now. But, on the spur of the moment, I left him.

Don What was it about?

Helen I beg your pardon?

Don The phone call.

Don turns his back on her for a moment, allowing her to worry about his next question

Was the phone call from Rosemary Mancini?

Helen's reaction shows clearly that Don is right

Helen I—I don't know ...

Don But, you left home because of it.

Helen Well ...

Don I must remind you—you're on oath.

Helen (*after a moment*) Yes—it was her! (*Clearly, she is very upset*)

Don And this was the cause of your argument?

She nods

Why should it upset you so much?

She does not answer

Did you know what their conversation was about?

Helen (*hesitantly*) No ...

Don Then why were you so upset?

Maggie (*interrupting*) Your Honour. Witness has said on oath that she doesn't know what the phone call was about.

Don Witness had to be reminded she was on oath. What was said on the phone might very well clear the prisoner of the suggestion that he was the father of Mrs Mancini's unborn child. (*He turns away from Maggie to appeal to Jane*)

Jane (*to Maggie*) I must allow the Defence to pursue this line of questioning. It could very well be that Mrs Mancini actually *named* the father of her child. And I think we should do everything possible to find out who it is. (*She turns her attention to Don, smiling*) So, I agree with the Defence.

Jane beams at Don, but clearly, he does not trust her. Having Jane on your

Act II

side is like going to bed with a viper. *Don moves closer to Helen, who is now very agitated*

Don (*sharply*) Do you still insist that you don't know what your husband and Rosemary Mancini talked about?
Helen (*faltering*) Yes . . .
Don Then I repeat—why were you so upset?
Helen I—I . . .
Don Why did you row with your husband? Why did you leave him?

Helen appears transfixed, unable to answer. Don goes to the desk and picks up the Bible. He moves back to Helen with it, and holds it up to her

You swore on oath on the Bible. I want to know *why—why* you were so upset. *Why* did you—
Maggie (*rising*) Your Honour—this is intimidation . . .

Don is not going to be stopped

Don (*continuing*) —fight with your husband? *Why* did you leave him? Was Joe having an affair with Rosemary? (*He rams the Bible right up under Helen's nose*)

Helen sags at the knees and collapses. Maggie moves quickly to her assistance. Liz gets to her feet and appears dumbstruck

Maggie Liz. Get some water. Quickly!

Liz seems transfixed

(*Shouting*) Liz!

Don joins Maggie

Liz (*coming out of her trance*) Yes . . . ?
Maggie Water!

Liz goes to a carafe of water on the dining table and pours some into a glass. Maggie "cradles" Helen in her lap. Liz goes to Maggie with the water. Don takes it and offers it to Helen, who drinks

Take it easy, love—it's all right . . .
Don (*angrily*) Are you going to call this off now?
Maggie (*angrily*) Is that why you did this to her? Hoping we'd give in?
Helen Maggie.
Maggie Don't worry, love. You won't have to answer any more questions.
Helen No, I want to tell you . . . (*She sits up*)
Maggie Don't worry about it . . .
Helen She wasn't the nice person you thought she was . . .
Maggie Rosemary had her faults—I know that.
Helen No—she was—bad. She tried to take Joe away from me.

There is a moment's pause

Maggie Are you trying to tell me it was Joe who made her pregnant?

Helen No, no. It wasn't him. (*Pause*) It all happened shortly after she came here. Not long before her husband went back to America. He told me what she was like. That's why they moved here—to get away from all the trouble she caused back home. It was meant to be a fresh start—except she started on Joe . . .

Helen is still upset. Maggie holds up the glass to her lips

Jane Counsel for the Defence. Do you wish to put any more questions to this witness?

Don No. I think there is sufficient doubt about my client's position with regard to Mrs Mancini's pregnancy. But, I would like to question him about his Sunday lunchtime meeting with Joe Francis.

Jane (*to Don*) Very well.

Don picks up the Bible and moves to Alan with it. He holds it so that Alan's handcuffed right hand is able to rest on it

Don Take the oath.

Alan I swear by Almighty God that the evidence I shall give will be the truth, the whole truth, and nothing but the truth.

Don returns the Bible to the desk and moves back to Alan

Don Were you responsible for Rosemary Mancini's condition?
Alan *I was not!*
Don Why did she ask you to approach Joe Francis on her behalf?
Alan She didn't ask. She told me to.
Don Told you to?
Alan Ordered me.
Don Will you explain.

There is a moment's pause as Alan considers

Alan She phoned me about eleven that Sunday morning and asked me to call round.
Don I see.
Alan She told me she was pregnant, and I told her she was a silly cow. I couldn't believe she wasn't on the Pill. Anyway, she *told* me to speak to Joe and persuade him to give her something. She'd tried earlier that morning and got nowhere.
Don Why you?
Alan Well, I refused at first—it was none of my business . . .
Don But—she told you . . .
Alan She'd been with me once when I was doing some business—it was during our "hot" period, which only lasted a few weeks. Anyway, I was offered—and I bought—some Georgian silver from a rather dubious source . . .
Don So she blackmailed you?

Maggie springs to her feet

Maggie Your Honour!

Act II

Jane (*to Don*) You will rephrase that question.

Again Jane gives him a sweet, sickly smile. It bothers him

Don (*to Alan*) So you were—given no choice.

Alan I got the distinct impression that if I didn't do as she asked I might have to explain a few things to the boys in blue.

Don So you went to see Joe.

Alan Yes. But, he was furious. I even offered him money. I was worried. I knew I didn't dare go back to Rosemary and tell her he wouldn't give me anything.

Don But, I am right in saying that he didn't give you something to—help—her?

Alan Abso-bloody-lutely! It put me in a right fix.

Don Are you saying that Mrs Mancini went to the police about your—business affairs—then?

Alan Oh, no. I couldn't have her doing that. When I left Joe, I nipped down into the town and found a little shop open. I bought a bottle of aspirins—soaked the label off—and told her to take three, four times a day.

Don (*tongue in cheek*) It didn't work, did it?

Alan (*smiling*) Apparently not.

Don But, you insist you had nothing to do with her condition?

Alan Yes I do.

Don Thank you. (*He turns to Maggie*) Do you wish to question the prisoner?

Maggie gets up and goes to the landing. When she gets there she consults her notes for a moment before confronting Alan

Maggie I must say—you mystify me.

Alan (*worried*) In what way?

Maggie I'll rephrase it. Your evidence mystifies me.

Alan (*warily*) Oh?

Maggie beams at him

Maggie (*to Alan*) Now you insist that you never had a relationship with Rosemary Mancini?

Alan I do.

Maggie *Once. Only once.* Is how you put it.

Alan I don't deny that occasion . . .

Maggie And yet just now—not more than two or three minutes ago you said—and I quote (*She reads from her notes*) "She'd been with me once when I was doing some business—it was during our 'hot' period, which only lasted for a few weeks."

Maggie looks up from her notes and smiles—a rather sickly smile—at Alan. His face tells all. He has dropped a monumental clanger. Don is furious

So—you had a "hot period" with the deceased which only lasted a few weeks. What d'you mean by that?

Alan looks and feels very uncomfortable

Alan Yes, but it was a long time ago. Nearly two years. Over the Christmas period . . .

Maggie So, it wasn't "just once. Only once"?

Alan Well, I did have an affair with Rosemary . . .

Maggie (*cutting in*) Oh, *you did*?

Alan I'm trying to explain . . .

Maggie Please do.

Alan It was only that one time this year.

Maggie First you say you didn't have a relationship with the deceased, then you say you did.

Alan Yes, but I meant nearly two years ago . . .

Maggie You meant nearly two years ago . . .

Alan Long before all this must have been brewing . . .

Maggie How convenient. I'm very intrigued by all you've been telling us. For instance, wouldn't you say that if a woman phones a man, asks him to call round to her house, tells him she's pregnant, asks him to help, they must be on reasonably intimate terms.

Alan Well—we were two of a kind, you know . . .

Maggie turns so that her back is towards him and appears to be contemplating: but, suddenly, she spins round to confront him, nostrils flaring

Maggie I put it to you that, *in fact*, Rosemary Mancini did not force you to approach Joe Francis. That, *in fact*, when she failed to persuade Joe, you followed up with an offer of a monetary bribe. That, *in fact*, the child she was carrying was not that of some phantom lover—but yours. *You* were responsible.

Alan No, no, no, no!

Maggie No?

Alan (*almost screaming*) No!

There is a moment's pause

Maggie On February the fourteenth, St Valentine's Day . . .

Alan (*realizing*) Oh, my God . . .

Maggie Yes, you need His help to get you out of this one. In this very house—or rather the garden shed—you had sexual intercourse with Rosemary Mancini. You were seen—by Jane Abbott. Is this true?

Alan is in a corner, a very tight corner. He does not quite know how to dodge the punches

Alan Well . . .

Maggie (*quickly*) And, on your own admission. If this is the case—and we do know that Rosemary was seeking an abortion on the twenty-second of March—well, I put it to you—what conclusions would you draw?

There is a pause. Alan bites his lip

Alan I didn't make love to her that evening

Act II

Another pause

Maggie (*shaking her head*) You didn't? But, earlier on you agreed that you had.
Alan Yes—but, only because I didn't want anyone to know . . .
Maggie You mean you haven't been entirely honest again?

Another awkward pause

Alan Well—I was in the garden shed with her—but . . .
Maggie But?

Alan looks extremely uncomfortable

Alan I—couldn't . . .
Maggie You—couldn't what?
Alan Make it. I'd had too much to drink. It was humiliating. She was in hysterics. Kept calling me—Limpy . . .
Liz Oh!
Maggie (*stifling a smile*) Limpy?
Alan For months afterwards. It's a wonder it didn't affect my performance permanently.
Maggie And you expect us to accept this *new* version as Gospel and that your previous offering was merely told to save you embarrassment?
Alan With my reputation, d'you really think I'd tell a lie about a thing like this?
Maggie You're proud of your reputation, are you?
Alan There's a lot of fellers on the estate who'd like it. D'you think I'd be prepared to jeopardize it—to make myself a laughing stock—if it wasn't the truth? 'Cos if you do—you don't know me!
Maggie And I don't want to—thank you very much! (*She turns to Jane*) Your Honour. I would like to call myself as a witness at this stage.
Jane (*to Helen*) Will you swear the witness in, please.

Maggie enters the Witness Box and Helen goes to her with the Bible. She holds it out and Maggie places her hand on it

Maggie I swear by Almighty God, that the evidence I shall give, will be the truth, the whole truth and nothing but the truth.

There is a moment's pause

If you remember I said I entered the deceased's house and found her lying dead on the bedroom floor. And you may recall I said earlier the photographs on the bed were *mostly* of her kids. I just kept looking through them. Then all of a sudden I realized I wasn't looking at photos of her children at all . . .

There is a longish awkward pause as they wait for her

The two photographs I held in my hands were of—the prisoner.

Don gets up, worried

Don This is the first time we've heard about these . .

Maggie puts her hand in the pocket of her gown and brings out two photographs

Maggie I have them here and I'd like to introduce them as evidence. You'll see that they are both of the prisoner and the deceased together. In one she is being kissed rather passionately by him—but, there's no mistaking them. And in the other he is holding her from behind with his hands clasped—in a very intimate manner—round her front.

Don takes the photos and looks at them

Alan I want to see those.
Maggie I've no objection.

Hesitantly, Don crosses to Alan and holds the photographs for him to look at them

Alan (*worried*) Well, er—we're always having parties—fun—you all know that. That's all it must have been—a bit of fun.
Jane I would like to see them.

Don hands the photos to Jane. She looks at them, then across at Alan—lethally

Thank you. Return them to the witness, please.

Helen does so

Maggie (*to Jane*) May I stand down, your Honour?
Jane Certainly.

Maggie comes out of the Witness Box and moves so that she is facing Alan. There is a moment between them—expectant, tense

Maggie I charge you again, Alan Edward Sexton, with the murder of Rosemary Mancini. In that on the twenty-third of June this year you knowingly and wilfully hung up on her when she phoned you for help. I am firmly of the opinion that the facts presented here today bear this out and can therefore leave no doubt in the Court's mind. One. You were seen entering the deceased's house—number nineteen Lock Close—not once, but twice—on the day she died. Two. You were known to be having an affair with her. Three. On the fourteenth of February, St Valentine's Day, you were seen making love to her in the garden shed of this house. Four. On the twenty-second of March you approached Joe Francis and tried to *bribe* him to help you procure an abortion for her. Five. On Wednesday the thirteenth of April you were seen in the company of the deceased by Jane Abbott and Don Parkes. Six ... (*She holds up the two photographs*) These two photographs show just how intimate your relationship was with the dead woman. And were found—where they had been placed in a moment of great distress—on the bed in her home ...
Alan You could still be lying about having found them on Rosemary's bed. I'd like to know who took those photographs.

Act II

Don steps in. He looks nervous—concerned

Don Your Honour. My client has a very good point. We can never actually know for certain that they were found on the deceased's bed. There's no way of corroborating it. And because of this, they should not be entered as evidence.

Alan suddenly becomes agitated

Alan I want to see them. I want to see them again.
Don It's not necessary. You've proved your point.
Alan I want to see them. They're of me. I want to see the bloody things.
Don They're not evidence any longer. There's no point.
Alan Whose side are you on?

There is a sharp moment between them

I think I've got something to say about them that might be needed as evidence. I want to see them.
Jane Let him see them.

Maggie says nothing—but, clearly, she is bothered by Alan's insistence. She goes to him and hands him the photographs—without a word. He looks at them—a smile of satisfaction on his face

Alan I remember. *Now I remember.* These were taken the Christmas before last. During my "hot" period with Rosemary. Here! In this very room. They're so close you'd hardly notice it. (*With a movement of his head he beckons Maggie to look at them*) Come here, have a look.

Maggie moves round and up on to the landing, where she looks over his shoulder

At the top of this one you can just make out the mistletoe. And on this other one you can see part of that oil lamp on the bookcase.

Throughout this Don clearly feels uncomfortable

Don The mistletoe proves nothing, Alan.

There is a moment's pause. Alan glares at him, then looks at the photographs

Alan But the oil lamp is the one I flogged you. *You* took these photographs . . .

There is a moment's pause. Maggie looks at Don, sensing his awkwardness

And *you*, Maggie. I'd lay odds that you dug them out of one of your drawers in the hope of getting everyone here to believe you found them at Rosemary's place. That's the truth—the real truth, isn't it?

There is a moment's pause. Without a word Maggie goes to the Bench, watched closely by the others, and Don in particular. She goes behind the Bench and opens one of the drawers in the lower half of the bookcase. There is a moment's pause. Then she comes out from behind the Bench and goes to Don, holding a large photograph album. Watched by the others, she carefully turns over the pages until she finds the one she is looking for. She holds it up for Don to look at. It is opened out so that two of the pages can be clearly seen. It is obvious that each page carries four photographs. On one of the pages two photographs are missing

Maggie (*coldly*) Who took them out of here?
Don (*after a brief hesitation*) I've no idea.
Maggie Who put them on Rosemary's bed?
Don I've no idea.
Alan You bastard. You rotten bastard. I've pulled some dirty ones in my time—but this. (*With a sudden thought*) Maggie. The key. That bloody key?
Maggie Key?
Alan It wouldn't fit—remember . . . ?

Maggie slips her hand into her pocket and produces the key. She holds it up, looking at it

In my trousers, Maggie. You'll find a bunch of keys. Get them.

Maggie crosses to his clothes on the Chesterfield. She searches in his trouser pockets and comes out with a bunch of keys. She goes to Alan, holding the keys out so that they can be seen

Liz was telling the truth—I always ask for a key. And I always keep it after we've finished. A memento . . .
Jane (*bitterly*) Scalps!

Alan gives her a quick worried glance

Alan No—a keepsake—that's all . . .

Maggie stands right by him with the keys

Maggie. The third one from the right. Match it up with the one you gave me.

Maggie does so

Are they the same?
Maggie (*flatly*) Yes.
Alan Well, that's the key to Rosemary's house.
Don Oh, come off it . . .
Alan If you don't believe me go along to number nineteen Lock Close and try it. (*His manner is full of conviction*)

Maggie moves to Don with the keys. They stand there facing each other. Clearly, Don is concerned and worried. Bitterness is welling up inside Maggie

Maggie Don't lie to me, Don. (*She holds out the single key*) Where did it come from?
Don How the hell should I know?
Maggie I tell you how. I found it in your *car*. You remember how filthy it was a little while back. I kept on at you to clean it. But, you didn't.

Act II

You left it for me to do as usual. I found this under the carpet. I suppose you must have dropped it. I thought it was our spare . . .
Don Oh, I don't want anything more to do with this—it's too ridiculous.
Maggie You deny any knowledge of it?
Don I do! I've never seen it before.

Maggie looks at Alan

Maggie Never tell them the truth, eh Alan? That's the last thing they want to hear.

Alan nods. There is a moment's pause

Alan I told you the quiet ones need watching. You tried to screw it for me, didn't you, Don? *My friend.* I suppose you figured that if there was any funny business over Rosemary they were more likely to come looking for *me* than anyone else. So you gave them a little help. Just to make sure no one suspected *you* . . .
Don Ridiculous. Bloody stupid!
Alan And it was me who told you about the *Red Stag* and The Links Motel. I remember telling you they didn't give a damn whether you stayed all night or not, so long as you paid your money.

Maggie turns to Jane

Maggie You lied, didn't you, Jane? It wasn't Alan you saw with Rosemary at the Links Motel. It was Don, wasn't it?

Jane says nothing, but her face reveals everything. Maggie moves closer to her, tense and bitter

And you knew very well he would back up your story, didn't you? He didn't have any choice. Because he suddenly realized your diary—your meticulously kept record—was of his meetings with Rosemary. But, that's the truth, isn't it?

Jane says nothing, and this is more than enough. Maggie turns her attention to Liz

And you, Liz. You're so bloody vain. The pretty lady. You weren't wearing your glasses when you were *supposed* to have seen Alan, were you?
Liz Well, I—could have sworn it was him . . . (*She trails off*)

Maggie moves to confront Don

Maggie (*very upset*) It was you Don, wasn't it?

Alan is full of cold fury. He interrupts Maggie

Alan (*to Don*) You dressed like me. You copied my walk . . . my mannerisms. Just in case someone saw you going into Rosemary's place.

Alan's head jerks round to look at Liz, who is clearly feeling terrible

And that stupid bird-brained bitch fell for it!

Liz stares at Alan for a moment—almost horrified, then hangs her head

Maggie (*to Don*) It was your baby she was expecting wasn't it? She threatened to tell me, didn't she! And now I come to think of it—she became very friendly with me for a while. That was your idea, wasn't it? But she was desperate to get you—that's why you hung up on her—isn't it?

Don Maggie—I swear to you I didn't hang up on her.

Maggie Please don't lie any more . . .

Don She phoned me at the office in the morning. Threatened me. Said she was going to take an overdose and leave a note explaining all about us. But I swear I didn't hang up on her.

Alan You rotten shit!

Without warning Maggie turns and dashes to the coffee table where she left the Spirits of Salt. She grabs the bottle and rushes back to Don, unscrewing the cap as she goes. Helen, the only one who realizes what is about to happen and, from keeping a very low profile, suddenly becomes active and hurls herself at Maggie, temporarily halting her

Helen Don't do it, Maggie. It'll burn his eyes out. Don't do it. He's telling the truth.

Maggie's momentum is fully checked. She stares incredulously at Helen

I hated her. I still do. She never left Joe alone. Even after she'd finished with him. And he was still crazy about her. D'you know what it's like to be in bed with someone when you know that they are thinking about someone else—knowing that they are pretending you are someone else. Anyway—that day, June the twenty-third, Joe had to play off a round in the Club championship. He left me in charge of the shop. I answered the phone to her. She thought Joe would know what to do. When I realized what she'd done and how far it had gone, I simply replaced the receiver. Just like that.

Don (*desperately*) You see, Maggie. You see. It wasn't me. I didn't put the phone down on her. I didn't leave her to die. I was telling the truth . . .

But, at this moment the telephone rings. It has the effect of "freezing" everybody. They don't quite know what to do about it. Except Liz, who looks blankly round at the others and then remembers her training. She'll always be a secretary! And consequently she assumes that everyone is waiting for her to answer it. She gets up and trots across as though nothing else of any importance is happening and answers it

Liz Riverside three-two-six-four. Mr and Mrs Parkes' residence. . . . Oh, well—I'm afraid Mr Parkes is rather tied up at this moment. . . . (*Then it occurs to her*) Well, we all are as a matter of fact. What did you say your name was? . . . Just a minute. (*She puts her hand over the telephone and addresses Don*) It's Herr Winkler from Cologne. He says you weren't on the plane.

Act II

The others are dumbfounded. Don edges across to the telephone. Liz hands it to him and crosses back to her position at the table

Don Parkes here. . . . Yes, I know that Herr Winkler—I'm very sorry. I can't explain now. But something's happened this end. I'll get back to you. . . . Thank you. Thank you very much.

He replaces the telephone and moves slowly back to Maggie and Helen

If only I hadn't forgotten that contract.
Maggie You didn't forget it.

She slips her hand inside her gown and produces the contract. She hands it to Don and in that instant he realizes all

Don Maggie . . .

But, before he can say any more, she hurls the contents of the chemist's bottle in his face. Both Don and Helen scream. Maggie is spent. Drained. She collapses into a chair. Then Don removes his hands from his face. Nothing has happened. Helen takes the bottle from Maggie and pours some of it into her hand

Helen It's water.
Maggie Just water. (*She looks up at Don*) But, he understands . . .

A pause

Helen (*to Maggie*) The key, love.

Maggie looks blankly at her

For the handcuffs.

Maggie gets the key out of her pocket and hands it to Helen. She crosses to Alan and releases him. Maggie and Don maintain their positions in silence. Helen finds her strength at last. She turns to the others and demands . . .

Helen What's the matter with all of you? Haven't you been given enough to think on? The show's over. Let's go!

Liz gets up and moves quickly out

Jane moves out from behind the Bench and moves to the door, dropping her gown en route. Here she stops and turns to give a last look to Alan, whose head drops. Then Helen and Alan exit together and in silence

A pause

Don We could have sorted this out together. It wasn't right this way, Maggie.
Maggie Right? Was it right the way you were—with Rosemary?
Don That was stupid. I tried to get out of it. You should have given me a chance to explain. It wasn't fair . . .
Maggie Or just?
Don No . . .

Maggie Let me remind you. When a woman talks about justice—she means retribution . . . You got what you deserved.

At this moment, Liz returns

They both turn to look at her

Liz Excuse me. I was wondering about next week's coffee morning.

Curtain

FURNITURE AND PROPERTY LIST

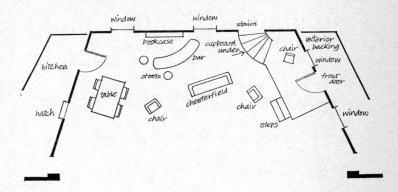

ACT I
SCENE 1

On stage: A heavy wrought-iron chair
Small Chesterfield
3 small chairs
Small dining-table. *On it:* tray, glass, milk jug, packet of bran, jar of honey, teaspoons
Coffee-table
Bookcase with various books including text-books and Bible. *In drawers under shelves:* camera, photograph album with 2 blank spaces. *On top:* oil lamp (not practical)
Small desk. *On it:* telephone, dressing
Bow-front mahogany chest with open back. *In back:* various drinks, including vodka, whisky, bottled orange, opened, various glasses. *On top:* open suitcase packed with clothing (no shirts) and dressing
2 high-backed bar stools
Hatch with ornamental shutter
Cupboard under stairs. *In it:* pile of clean laundry, poker
Coat stand. *On it:* raincoat, **Don**'s jacket
Carpet. *Under it:* length of electric cable with socket on one end
Window curtains

Off stage: Several clean shirts (**Maggie**)
Length of electric cable with plug attached (**Maggie**)
Suitcase. *In it:* prison jacket and trousers, 2 pairs of handcuffs with key (**Maggie**)

Personal: **Maggie:** wristwatch, barrister's wig and gown, handbag with mirror, cold cream, tissues, hairpins
Alan: St Christopher medallion, doorkey, bunch of keys
Jane: barrister's wig and gown
Helen: barrister's wig and gown
Liz: barrister's wig and gown, spectacles

Scene 2

Set: Cut-out dock
Witness Box
Table, chairs and desk arranged to represent Court
On desk: pads, pencils, folders, briefcase with loose-leaf folder and papers
On "Bench": gavel, block
On breakfast counter (concealed from sight): Variable Mains Dropper
On dining-table: carafe of water, glass

Off stage: Chemist's brown bottle containing water (**Maggie**)

Personal: **Jane:** High Court Judge regalia

ACT II

Set: Variable Mains Dropper on Bench

Off stage: Clipboard with papers and pencil (**Don**)

Personal: **Jane:** diary
Maggie: 2 photographs, key

LIGHTING PLOT

Practical fittings required: wall brackets, spotlights
Interior: A living-room and dining-room. The same scene throughout

ACT I. SCENE 1 Morning
To open: General effect of morning light
No cues

CURTAIN

ACT I. SCENE 2 Morning
To open: Curtains closed. Daylight outside. All practicals on
No cues

CURTAIN.

ACT II As close of previous scene
No cues

BOWS
CURTAIN.

EFFECTS PLOT

ACT I
Scene 1

Cue 1	**Don:** "... anyone who crosses you." *Doorbell rings*	(Page 8)
Cue 2	**Don:** "She recognized poor Helen..." *Taxi approaches, stops, horn sounds*	(Page 10)
Cue 3	**Maggie** replaces cable under carpet *Doorbell rings*	(Page 11)

Scene 2

No cues

ACT II

Cue 4	**Don:** "I was telling the truth..." *Telephone rings*	(Page 68)

MADE AND PRINTED IN GREAT BRITAIN BY
LATIMER TREND & COMPANY LTD PLYMOUTH
MADE IN ENGLAND

DRAMA COLLECTION
WITHAM LIBRARY
18, NEWLAND STREET
WITHAM
ESSEX, CM8 2AQ

14. DEC. 1981	18. AUG. 1986	
-1. NOV. 1982		
-2. DEC. 1982	14. JUL. 1987	
-4. FEB. 1983	11. FEB. 1988	
-1 MAY 1983		
31. AUG. 1983	11. MAR. 1989	
31 JAN 1984	14 APR 1989	
29. MAY 1984	15 JUL 1991	
25 SEP 1984	27 AUG 1991	
18. JUL.		

822.914
DARBON L
Time to kill.
a play

CX61159

822.914	ACC. No.	CX61159
DARBON L		Time to kill. a play

ESSEX COUNTY LIBRARY
H.Q. BIB: SERVICES .... LIBRARY

DRAMA SECTION

This book is to be returned on or before the last date above.
It may be borrowed for a further period if not in demand.